Escape From Bondage

A Remarkable Escape From the Point of No Return

Mahlon F. Harris

TEACH Services, Inc.
PUBLISHING
www.TEACHServices.com • (800) 367-1844

World rights reserved. This book or any portion thereof may not be copied or reproduced in any form or manner whatever, except as provided by law, without the written permission of the publisher, except by a reviewer who may quote brief passages in a review.

This book was written to provide truthful information in regard to the subject matter covered. The author assumes full responsibility for the accuracy of all facts and quotations as cited in this book. The opinions expressed in this book are the author's personal views and interpretation of the Bible, Spirit of Prophecy, and/or contemporary authors and do not necessarily reflect those of TEACH Services, Inc.

This book is sold with the understanding that the publisher is not engaged in giving spiritual, legal, medical, or other professional advice. If authoritative advice is needed, the reader should seek the counsel of a competent professional.

Cover Photograph and Author Portrait by Liesl Harris Clark

Copyright © 2013 TEACH Services, Inc.
ISBN-13: 978-1-4796-0047-2 (Paperback)
ISBN-13: 978-1-4796-0048-9 (ePub)
ISBN-13: 978-1-4796-0049-6 (Kindle/Mobi)

Library of Congress Control Number: 2013933167

Published by

TEACH Services, Inc.
P U B L I S H I N G
www.TEACHServices.com • (800) 367-1844

Foreword

Escape from Bondage will keep you turning pages late into the night. This book does much more than tell a story, it allows us into the mind and soul of a man who has a brain attack—and survives to live with the results of his stroke.

The author, Mahlon F. Harris, writes from within his own experience, using Harry Tucker's story to share the desperate hopes he has heard and felt with the patients he has cared for over the years.

This is a very personal book, telling stories that are so impossible they have to be true. Stop and listen as you read. Chances are you will hear your own heart beating in time with Harry Tucker's, feel the sweat of his desperation, and the joy of his tears.

Numerous research studies have confirmed that the power of Faith in God is equal or superior to the effect of many modern medications. Harris, in telling Harry's stories, reaffirms that truth. He also demonstrates the unique power that God-fearing caregivers bring to their work. Alone, we lose hope. Together with God, impossible dreams become reality.

I have joined the HK Club and make certain my life leaves at least as many good memories as the folks in this tale.

As you read, please listen closely to Kathy, to Harry, to the kids, and to Queen Lillian. Their story—all the very best parts—can be yours.

—Dick Duerksen
Storyteller
Maranatha Volunteers International
www.maranatha.org

Chapter One

~~~

Finally, Harry Tucker identified the people encircling his bed: the head nurse, physical therapist, the attending physician, Thomas, and his attorney. Each person's voice sounded like static: coarse, gritty, and rough. As hard as Harry tried to focus on their conversation, their frequent agitation and impatience prevented comprehension. A statement made by one of the team riled him. But when he tried to express his displeasure, his pasty and immobile mouth could not deliver the words. He could not utter a sound. Then the entire group abruptly turned and exited without so much as a backward glance, except for the lady with raven-colored hair. She cast a lingering glance at his distorted face, and then she, too, was gone.

Questions began forming in Harry's mind, a confused tumbling of thoughts. Because his head would not obey, he rolled his eyes about to get his bearings. As he nervously cast about the room, he squinted in the glare of the chandelier hanging from a light-colored ceiling. Out of the corner of his left eye, he made out the blurred shape of a small table on which appeared to be some kind of blue object. Beyond that he saw a faded yellow wall. To the right a curtain with smudges and folds cascaded from the ceiling to below his bedside. His mind struggled to keep pace with his roving eyes. He identified the bottom of a bed beyond his bare feet. And then he saw the opening, a curtain perhaps, through which moving objects occasionally passed.

Harry's eyes snapped shut from the exertion, but he willed them to obey his command to re-open and investigate the scene around him. Yes! There was a doorway. Yes! The moving shapes were busy people.

As Harry slowly relaxed his tense eye muscles and tried to figure out what was going on, he became aware of a constant pressure inside his head that screamed for release. Such pain! He tried lifting his hands to rub his head. The right hand moved slowly toward his face. But where was his left hand? His head writhed inside the vise that gripped it as his eyes searched for his left hand. Sweating slightly from the exertion, he relaxed his uncooperative muscles and pondered his predicament while his left hand was nowhere in sight.

Harry heard a bustling sound, and then a form passed through the doorway and floated to his bedside. A woman's voice said, "How are we today, Harry?"

Margaret? No.

When she saw him blink, she repeated her question, adding, "I see we have our eyes open. How do we feel? Would we like a drink of fresh water?" He felt the dry skin of a cool and delicate hand on his head.

Who is this? he thought. *My secretary? Daughter? Wife ... Margaret? Is she still my wife? No, I don't have a wife anymore.*

Although her hand did not stay in one place very long, Harry sensed her caring. He later dubbed her Lady Lightning for she seemed always in a hurry.

"Suck on the straw, Harry!" she shouted.

Hmmm ... She seems to know me, but why is she shouting? Do I know her? He felt cool liquid on his tongue and in his mouth.

"Swallow!" Lady Lightning shouted.

Why does she yell? he thought. His irritation flowed over his tongue and down his throat with the cool fluid. Then he felt the trail of moisture trickling on his chest directly under his chin, around his neck, and down his right side.

"Have some more!" On her command, Harry again pursed his lips and pulled the liquid through the straw.

Is she pressing my lips together? Harry wondered. Not as much fluid escaped this time.

Harry's focus finally clicked in. She was smiling, a really nice smile. So he said, "Gaba. Baa. Kawaka. Dawdaw!"

She did not seem to understand him, so he rephrased: "Fafa. Mana. Kawkaw." Her puzzled expression increased his anxiety. His words were not making sense to this person, or to him. She frowned, turned, and glided out the door.

Now Harry was sweating buckets. He put his right hand on his face to give it a once-over and he mentally took inventory. *OK! Two eyes. One nose. Two ears ... one ear? What happened to the left ear? There's skin on the right side. But what had happened to the skin on the left side? Oh my! My mouth feels puckered! It's sagging on the left side! Where is that woman dressed in white?*

The vise had loosened its grip on Harry's head. He could move it enough to see down both sides of his body, although not very clearly on the left side. He saw a stainless steel pole with a plastic bag hanging from it. He followed the plastic tubing until it reached his arm. *That's it*, he thought, *they have the arm secured for some reason. The hand has been ... cut off?* He tried to remember what had happened. *Why am I here?* His mind formed a scream, *Where is that woman?* But only garbled words tumbled from his puckered mouth.

So he talked to himself within himself: *Am I dreaming? No, this is a nightmare! OK! OK! Relax! Breathe deeply! Isn't that how I have counseled others in times past?*

Harry continued to think through the experience. *I am in ... a hospital room. Yes, that's it! But why would I be in a hospital, moreover, in a hospital bed? I cannot move parts of my body. I cannot speak coherently. There are tubes and nurses. What is wrong with me? Why am I here? Why am I here? Where is Heather? Oh, she's in Europe studying and performing. How long have I been here? Didn't she wonder why I had not written or called? Certainly she has been in touch with Thomas. He would have told her about me. Or would he? When she returns home, will she ever be able to find me?* He clutched his nightshirt to choke back the thoughts that terrorized him. Then he paced his thinking more slowly.

Chapter Two

―⸺☙ ❧⸺―

Several weeks passed. As Harry Tucker lay in his bed, he struggled to put together fragments of his life as thoughts began to surface and swirl within his aching brain. Now he remembered that he worked with doctors, so he tried to recall what questions doctors asked patients to determine their grip on reality. He interviewed himself.

Date of birth: *October 10, 1954.*

Life events: Harry reigned in his wandering thoughts to review what he could remember of his life.

I am a businessman who owns and manages a medical clinical laboratory with several satellite draw stations. Harry thought of the endless amount of energy required to get them functioning efficiently. He remembered his work was no longer demanding because he had hired wisely and had qualified people in key departments. *But being a workaholic and a conscientious person, I go to my office daily to make sure all systems (functional as well as technical) maintain exceptionally high standards. I had entertained thoughts of slowing down, perhaps even retiring. Someday. I'm too young. I am happy and reasonably content. I've seen too many people retire early thinking to escape the rat race. But after retirement, without structure and responsibilities, they sat around, watched television, grew fat and lazy, then died early.* More and more he thought of putting his skills to work for volunteer health care organizations in developing countries. He had taken several short-term overseas trips and found humanitarianism to be very rewarding and fulfilling. His family would not care. He was sure of that.

My family. Hmmm ... Margaret? Now he remembered some things about her. They had married when they were both very young, hot-headed, and impulsive. Margaret really was not what you could call a wife anymore. Actually, she had never been much of a homemaker either.

He had been reticent to believe the rumors that had circulated shortly after their honeymoon, that she was cavorting with former male friends. He had hoped that after little Tommy was born... *Tommy? Yes, I have a son.* He had hoped Tommy's birth would make things different. Their relationship did seem to improve. Twenty-six months after Tommy was born, little Heather arrived.

The thought of his loving Heather made his heart ache. Margaret, at first, objected to having another child, but she soon seemed to accept sweet, serene Heather.

Harry recalled that as endless activities and responsibilities pressed in on their marriage, his relationship with Margaret turned downward again. While he had learned to accept and shoulder responsibilities and to honor commitment, she had not. Margaret began spending more and more time away from home, often returning very late at night and sometimes not until the next day.

Just remembering tied his heart in knots. *I tried to appreciate her desire to maintain some semblance of her home decorating career. After all, hadn't she accepted my long hours and determination to build a business? But I did wonder what households would require late night or all-night decorating consultations. I made sure that I was always home from work in time to eat supper with the children, to play with them a while before reading bed-time stories, and to listen to their good-night prayers. Mrs. Wilson, the nanny, certainly did not replace the children's mother, but she was very good with them and they loved her dearly. She was a Christian who possessed grandmotherly love and gentleness. So, the environment for the children, while perhaps not perfect, was secure and loving.*

Gradually, Margaret's interior design enterprise had developed into a highly regarded full-time business. Her clients and friends became her family. Following Heather's third birthday party, she hardly ever returned home. She had leased a posh suite hundreds of miles away in a four star hotel. She was very talented and her abilities were in demand.

I remember the last time I saw Margaret. She had invited me to attend an awards ceremony where she was to be honored for exquisitely decorating a well-known millionaire's penthouse. I normally shied away from such gatherings. But this was a tremendous honor for her, and I wanted to show my support. What an evening! There were speeches, awards, toasts and proclamations of good will and health. On and on! Margaret, the social butterfly, flitted from table to table, noticing everyone except me. I got tired of it! I went to bed in Margaret's suite. Hours later she had slipped into bed beside me. Her breath, her slurred speech, and her behavior was different from the Margaret I knew. Before we could talk about the events of the evening, someone began banging on our door! Immediately Margaret got out of bed and put on her robe. Through the partially opened door in the living room, I heard their whispers. One of Margaret's materials suppliers had dropped by to get his "commission." I did not want to acknowledge that her body had become part of her business assets.

By the time Tommy and Heather graduated from high school, the frequency of their mother's home visits was so rare and her contacts so few that they expressed little affection for her. An occasional telephone call and a less occasional written note or card was seldom even mentioned by either of the children. They had developed their own friends and had filled the vacuum with their own agendas. Heather developed skills in fine arts, concentrating on piano and voice. Harry sighed. The bond linking Heather to me grew stronger, while there was increasingly less common ground between Tommy and me. This was odd, because Tommy had developed the same aggressive business characteristics I had displayed at his age. Harry would later learn that Tommy's developing over-aggressive behavior had a direct link to his mother's lack of love and attention during his childhood.

Harry learned now that he was the victim of a cerebral vascular accident (CVA), also known as stroke or brain attack. This was one of his worst fears. He realized that he must have been in this state for some time, but how long he was not sure. Maybe it was only a few weeks, maybe for many months. He remembered that his mother and an older brother had suffered from strokes. His mother had rehabilitated. But his brother had debilitated, soon suffering a heart attack and dying at 42, Harry's age.

Having been in the health care profession for many years, Harry had witnessed patients who so much wanted to speak but could not get the words out. Confusion, embarrassment, and extreme sadness generally culminated in tears. As he lay on his bed, not being able to speak or move his left arm or left leg, he became more and more unhappy. He recalled that with fast medical intervention, many people with a stroke can quickly rehabilitate (see appendix C). With his limited ability to process the extent of his symptoms, he concentrated on trying to ascertain if he was in this place to rehabilitate or vegetate.

Harry Tucker pieced together incidents that had undoubtedly led up to this brain attack. Tag O'Reilly and his assistant Jeremy were in his office again, just one of multiple visits. Coastal Medical had made several propositions to acquire Harry's corporation. He had been vacillating, concerned about what to do if he did not have this business. He needed organization and regimen. He had a few hobbies, but he needed some definite daily activities. He liked the feeling of fulfillment in providing superior service to patients and professionals who depended on him and with whom he had built a very respectable relationship. He replayed the scene.

"Well, Harry, when are you going to take that time off you have been promising yourself?" Tag had pressed for an answer. "Aren't you getting to the age when you should be doing things for yourself? You know, for the amount of money we're offering for your corporation, you could retire, travel, play golf, or sit by the pool drinking lemonade and enjoying the company of young maidens heeding your every beck and call."

At least some of that scenario had sounded good to Harry. He could travel to Paris where Heather was advancing her studies in music. She and a few friends had formed a singing group, and they were performing in various cities throughout Europe and England. He could spend time with Tommy, that is, if he could spare the time for his dad.

His businesses and business deals were taking so much of his time that he had little left for himself, let alone his dad.

Actually, they were both guilty, Harry admitted that to himself. *Do I really know the person Tommy has become?*

"Have you some questions about my proposal?" Tag's question brought Harry back to the present.

"I'll have to give it more thought," Harry replied. He knew Tag understood he was putting him off again.

Tag and Jeremy soon left with the usual parting words, "Call me." Harry knew he would not. But Tag was persistent. He would be back.

As Harry stood to shake hands, he suddenly felt a little dizzy. The men left, and he slumped into a chair. At the same time, the lights in the room seemed very bright, and a metallic taste coated his tongue. He glanced out the window. Such a wonderful view! He always enjoyed it. He so often gazed out upon the green grass with the beautifully sculptured shrubs and manicured lawns surrounding his office. He learned to sculpt shrubs on a business trip to the Far East where Mr. Lin, a Chinese gardener, had given him lessons.

The familiar scenery did not produce the usual calming effect. There seemed to be something covering his vision, a jagged kaleidoscopic streak going from left to right, or was it right to left and sometimes in circles? He blinked, and blinked again. He breathed in deeply, exhaling slowly. He tried focusing on different objects. He remembered feeling weaker and lying down, thinking he must have a touch of the flu. Then the scene changed. He was lying flat in a bed, and people were standing around talking about him.

He later learned the facts. About thirty minutes after Tag left, Brenda, his secretary, paged him on the intercom for a telephone call. After several unanswered attempts, she entered his office and found him sprawled on the sofa, unconscious.

Brenda had called an ambulance. Later he was told that at the hospital he had been given blood tests, a Computerized Axial Tomography (CAT Scan), a Magnetic Resonance Imaging (MRI), and a Magnetic Resonance Angiography (MRA), special procedures including heart and other catheterizations, poking and prodding, needles and tubes. He had not been conscious during all of this. The morning he awoke to see those people standing around his bed had been his first bit of consciousness for more than six months.

Now his predicament gradually became reality. He was flat on his back and did not have normal body functions. His right leg and arm, though weak, seemed normal. He could move them with some degree of dexterity. But his left extremities, the entire left side of his body, was numb. He fought off panic by trying to relax, talking himself through the fog that tried to envelop him as he checked off the damage. He could not talk. He could barely swallow. He could turn his head but only slightly and with difficulty. Eventually his mind won out, and he screamed inside: *I am a shell! I'm half a human, half dead, half alive! I'm a bag of bones and protoplasm!*

"How are we today?" The nurse's voice interrupted his silent screaming. Yet he thought to himself, *I don't know how* you *are, but I am definitely not good.* When he tried to respond politely, he heard himself say, "Awwhgaa."

"Oh, that's good." she replied. "I see we are awake now. Lunch will be here soon."

We? he grumbled within himself. *Don't I have a name? Lunch? Who could eat lunch?*

Harry had not eaten solid food during the many weeks he had been in a coma. Intravenous and stomach feedings had kept him alive. The aromas coming from the hallway did something to his stomach, but they were not causing hunger. The nurse, evidently finishing her observation of him, patted his arm, smiled ever so sweetly, and waltzed away.

Alone again, Harry complained to himself, *I do not want to be alone.* This was a relatively new sensation. A shy man, Harry had always kept to himself. But now he wanted someone near, someone to touch, someone to touch him, someone to break the deafening silence of his horizontal world. He needed to hear someone say, "You're going to be all right, Harry," even if it was not the truth. He could not understand his own speech, so to hear another voice would have been comforting. He felt so alone. *Do I have any true friends?* he wondered. *Where are they? Where is God? Isn't He supposed to be near at a time like this?*

Even then Harry admitted to himself that God had not forsaken him. *I've moved away from God. He is waiting for me to renew our relationship. But did He need to go to this much trouble?*

Harry had a lot of time to think, and often his thoughts turned to God. One thought kept pressing for attention. *God created me. He knows what has happened to my body and He can fix it.* Harry had the awareness that he was not in this thing alone. *He is with me. Doesn't the Good Book say, "I will never forsake you"?* he asked himself.

A few days after Harry had regained consciousness, his attending physician recommended resuming physical therapy and beginning speech therapy. Harry later learned he had had limited physical therapy at the rehabilitation hospital to help prevent complete muscle atrophy. He had been hospitalized the majority of the time since his stroke prior to his admission to this facility several weeks ago. To Harry's surprise and delight, the raven-haired lady he had seen that first day was going to be his rehabilitation physical therapist.

"Good morning, Mr. Tucker. I am happy to see that you have awakened from your long sleep. I have looked in on you nearly every day hoping you would regain consciousness soon. My name is Kathy, and I'm your physical therapist. We need to get your weakened muscles and tired, stiff bones moving again. It will hurt a little, because it's been a long time since you have experienced physical activity. I'll go slowly."

The first non-condescending voice I've heard, Harry reflected.

"Your nurse told me you do not speak yet, Harry, so keep your eyes turned toward me. That way I can interpret your facial expressions to know if you hear me or if you have arrived at your limit of therapy tolerance. OK?" She continued as if she did not expect a response from him. But Harry was busy with his own thoughts anyway. *Is there hope*? he wondered.

The first day of therapy was traumatic. Flex the leg, extend the leg. Flex the arm, extend the arm and on and on and on. Muscles, ligaments, skin, and other anatomy that had been at rest he did not know for how long, vehemently resisted. Days and days passed with the same succession of exercises, especially to the left side. By now his good nature had been stretched and extended to the limit as well. But about the fourth week, his mind became a little more active and now he focused more on Kathy. Even though his movements were always with some degree of pain, he watched this woman intently. She stopped when he winced. Kathy was caring and seemed to really enjoy her work. She labored as though what she was doing was going to pay off for him, and she could hardly wait to see the results. Her optimism could be felt. He could not verbally communicate with her, but he so much wanted to return her nice warm, encouraging smile. He wanted to get up and walk if for no other reason than to prevent that fleeting look of disappointment crossing her pretty face.

The preliminary in-bed exercises continued daily for weeks. While it could not be proven by him, the physical therapist said she could feel the muscles strengthening. *Some optimism this woman has*, he thought. The morning she announced she was going to set him up on the side of his bed, his heart raced.

"Maybe we'll even have you stand on your feet," she said. "We will see how it goes with the sitting position first." When Harry's croaking resounded, Kathy raised her eyebrows and mentally noted that Harry's impaired hearing had improved.

Paying little heed to Harry's objections, Kathy proceeded to place one determined arm under his shoulders and her hand firmly under his knees. With one graceful, fluid movement, the experienced therapist slowly and effortlessly guided him to a sitting position on the side of his bed.

Whoa! Harry wished he could express his excitement. After having reclined for so long during most of his hospitalization, the new position simultaneously produced lightheadedness, sweating, and nausea. The room moved erratically. Dark clouds first enveloped him and then receded. Harry felt embarrassingly shaky. Acutely aware that his left arm was useless, Harry frantically groped for something secure with his right hand. The bed rail was down, so he could not clutch it. Grabbing the bed linens only loosened them. The pillow fell to the floor, and sheets balled around him. Feeling helpless and hopeless, Harry heard a soothing voice saying, "You're OK. You're OK, Mr. Tucker. Take it easy now."

As the dizziness passed, the wobbling decreased, and Harry's sense of balance slowly returned, he discovered his good arm was tightly around the therapist's shoulders. Equilibrium had been his primary goal to be sure, but here he was in the firm embrace of a person, gender being immaterial for the moment. His psyche craved the human touch. This felt so good, his arm around Kathy's solid body, and her holding him securely. He wanted to savor this moment of human contact. But his otherwise slow brain reacted, and he jerked away, sending himself into another ungraceful balancing act.

"Relax, friend, relax" Kathy soothed Harry. "Just go slow and easy. Don't get overly excited. You haven't been upright for a long time. It's normal to be dizzy and to feel insecure. Just hold on to me a moment. I'll hold you quietly until the dizziness passes."

Safe within his mental dialogue, Harry admitted, *Actually, I'm in no hurry to be out of your clutches, lady.*

He tried to relax, to let his head press against her shoulder as she firmly held him upright. The brief contact warmed his heart, but his code of ethics compelled him to pull away. To his surprise, Kathy held him tightly with a steady hand.

"Let your feet slide to the floor, Harry."

She's a professional! Harry scolded himself but was not sure why he was so frenzied about the matter. *Maybe I'm embarrassed to need to be comforted.* Yet, he was standing! So he focused on this landmark accomplishment, leaning against the therapist in front with the bed behind him. Kathy repeated this routine twice a day for several days.

The second week while he sat on the side of his bed waiting for his equilibrium to stabilize, he noticed a brace lying in the wheelchair. As though the therapist was reading his mind, she said, "The brace has been sized and adjusted to fit your paralyzed leg, Harry. It'll provide the stiffness and straightness you need to bear your weight," Kathy explained. Brandishing a cane with several short legs, she added, "And this has been adjusted for your use." Kathy assisted him into his wheelchair and pushed him to the physical therapy department.

Harry was apprehensive about embarking on this new venture. Kathy pushed his wheelchair to an open door, over the top of which he noticed a suspended pulley. Through the pulley passed a rope with pieces of Velcro attached to either end. She locked the wheels of his wheelchair and secured his hands in the stirrups with the pieces of Velcro. "I will continue with your leg exercises, Harry, but this device will enable you to strengthen your arms. With your good, right hand pull down on this rope, and your left arm will raise. Ease up on the right side, Harry, and the weight of your left arm will let it go down while pulling the right arm up. Let your arms go up and down, up and down, for as long as you can, but rest as often as you wish. Show me what you can do."

He did it. Not very coordinated at first, however. His rhythm smoothed and she said, "I'd like you to work at this for an hour. While you are working out, I will go and get another patient to treat." She made sure he was securely fastened in his chair and left to get her next scheduled patient.

After only a few minutes of this pull-down-and-let-up routine, Harry's arm muscles begged for relief. He thought this was probably a good sign. Harry did the leg exercises for the next two weeks.

One morning Kathy entered his room, smiling. She announced she was going to "walk him." *Yeah, right*, Harry chuckled to himself. Harry's left leg felt completely dead, no feeling at all. Without looking, Harry could not tell where the leg was at any given moment. *Although Kathy is very patient, how could one small person handle a tall man like me?* he thought. Kathy, in her usual confident manner, told him how to lean on his right leg and swing the left leg forward. "Just a little to begin with," she said. She encouraged him by talking quietly, never raising her voice.

"Being upright will feel very strange to you, Harry. Like many of my other patients, your leg feels numb. You feel insecure. And you are afraid to move." She used short phrases, pausing between each, waiting for his mind to catch up.

"When you were beginning to walk as a child, you learned balance by first getting onto your hands and knees, and then after a while you began to crawl. Then you pulled yourself up and held onto an object for support, wobbling, teetering, and then falling. Over and over you tried until your brain developed knowledge and your legs grew stronger. As you developed balance and your muscles strengthened, you took your first step. You have to learn to walk all over again, Harry. We'll bypass the crawling stage," she said with a twinkle in her eyes. Harry's brain agreed with her reasoning, but his emotions wavered.

Kathy continued, "Through your teenage and early adult years you were constantly learning balance and coordination. Now you are learning again. Perhaps this time from a different perspective, but the brain is going to start the process again. Be cautious. Be patient. Be determined, Harry!" Her soft voice gently raised was full of spunk. Harry's fear remained.

"I will stand in front of you," Kathy assured Harry. "I'll have my arms under your arms. Lean toward me but not on me, unless you feel you are going to fall. If you do feel you are going to fall, let the cane drop and come to me." She stood quietly, giving Harry a minute to process all of this. Then she spoke. "Ready, Harry? Your good hand is on the cane. My arms are under yours. Now lean forward away from the bed." She helped him.

Did I wiggle forward? The pace of Harry's mental conversation was rapid. His mind was in high gear, and his heart raced.

"Stand still without moving for just a minute," Kathy ordered. Harry gratefully obeyed. He was already tired. He was swaying and sweating. His muscles were trembling like an aspen leaf in the wind. Kathy had noticed all his physical responses, but she didn't mention any of them. "Easy now," she said softly. "Slowly shift your weight to the right. That's good. You are doing fine." Harry's heart thundered a drum roll of self-praise as Kathy guided him physically and verbally. "I'll step back slightly, and while you lean on the right leg, swing the left leg forward." As Harry took a small step forward, his left leg swung too far. He lost his balance and he panicked.

Harry could hardly remember getting back into bed. Yet Kathy praised his two-minute lunging and thrashing affair. However, a defeatist attitude momentarily surfaced within him, saying, *I'll never be able to walk.* And he would have told her as much if he could speak.

Harry melted into the bed. Covered with perspiration, his muscles quavered and his heart thumped a John Philip Sousa march. Kathy had anticipated the effect of this first effort to walk. She wiped the sweat from his face and cooled his brow with a damp cloth, assuring him with words of hope and confidence. She wiped his face again, smiled, and excused herself to go treat another resident. A discouraged Harry could only lie in bed, panting and perspiring profusely.

Chapter Three

─⊰ ⊱─

Another sleepless night. *Another Harry Tucker night*, he thought as he lay in bed, mentally balancing his accounts. *Why must I suffer with this debilitating infirmity? I'm an honest businessman. I'm generous. I give money to many organizations and needy people. I'm financially secure. I've lived a pretty good life, considering. Just when I was thinking of slowing down and relaxing my work schedule to have more time for myself, this happens! Why?*

A thought kept creeping into his mind. It threatened to drown him. *It's that God thing*, he finally admitted to himself. *I've developed a suitable respect for the Manager of the Universe—neither too close nor too distant. But I've been the only one comfortable with our relationship, that loose connection with Him. I need something more than science or medicine can provide. I need healing! I need a miracle! Will God allow it?*

Harry reviewed his childhood religion and snatches of "religion on the street," as he called it. He had heard one time that a man could keep the Creator far enough away to keep Him from interfering with his plans but close enough so that God could be called on in case of emergency. *Yet I'm months into this mess, and I've just now thought about involving God!* Harry chastised himself. Then he tried to appease himself. *They say that man's extremity is God's opportunity! And I'm about as far to the extreme as I can get.*

Mental sparring had become Harry's all-consuming activity every day. He retold himself the stories he had learned as a child and had shared with his own children. The stories of Daniel had always fascinated him and his children. *How does that story go?* Harry searched through his mental library. Hananiah, Mishel, and Azariah were taken captive by Nebuchadnezzar at the conquest of Jerusalem to be enslaved in labor in the Babylonian President's marble White House. Daniel and his friends were given Arab names of Belteshazzar, Shadrach, Meshach and Abednego.

Because these young men were being schooled to work in top-level government matters, they were served richer and more refined foods than the common slave trainees.

Daniel and his friends were not accustomed to the rich foods on the ruler's table, so they requested a simple diet of plain foods. How brave and courageous Daniel and his colleagues had been to suggest they knew better eating practices than those of the king of Babylon. *Now what was so special about them that they should have been allowed to have a special diet,* Harry mused. *They seemed to be a cut above the others, so they were permitted special privileges. But they were slaves!* His mind could scarcely contain his bellowing. *Yet they had the audacity to request a special diet!*

Harry's mind drifted to a time and place when he had a special food prepared for him. He was in the Philippines helping refugees from war-torn countries when some island residents treated him and his friends to a local delicacy. "Neelapok" was what the name of the concoction sounded like. It was fresh banana and fresh coconut beaten together and served on a banana leaf. He remembered how they had joked about the banana leaf being the "special dish."

Harry also remembered the stories he had heard about the advantages of healthful eating habits and exercise. If translated, his mumblings would be, "*It seems like the Good Book with its stories and instructions gives people just what they need to live a long and happy life.*" His memory was awakening with more and more facts on the subject of health as he considered how those facts might positively impact his present condition. He recalled the ingredients of the original plan for happy living. *Maybe it's not too late to begin,* his silent voice urged. With thoughts of what might be required of him to regain health and a plan he could put into action, he sank into a peaceful sleep dreaming of daring to be a Daniel.

The next day after lunch Harry was transferred from his bed to the wheelchair and scuttled close to the nurses' station. This location made it easier for the nurses to keep an eye on this newcomer who had recently awakened from a long coma. This position also gave Harry a bird's eye view of the goings on of other residents. It allowed him to observe the nurses and nursing assistants too.

Sitting across the hall was a man who looked to Harry to be in similar shape as him. Although he was tied into his wheelchair, he had a brace on an arm and a leg. He was trying to get someone's attention, but his attempts to verbalize sounded like Harry's own jabbering.

The man wailed continuously. "Bee! Bee!" A couple of aides came by. One said, "Get you in a minute, Pete," but hurried down the hall. The man began erratically waving the unbraced arm. Although his words were indistinguishable, the sounds were clearly uncomplimentary. Yet the staff played a broken record, "In a minute, Pete." Moments later Harry glanced at Pete, who seemed to have gathered a very self-satisfied smirk to his lopsided face. Then Harry heard the drip-drip-drip and then saw yellow liquid pooling beneath Pete's wheelchair. Harry looked up to see Pete watching him, wearing a clearly recognizable "I told you so" expression on his misshapen face. An aide sauntering by inadvertently scuffed the water, which splattered onto her ankle. Sliding to avoid doing the splits in mid-corridor, she executed a series of ungraceful calisthenics to avoid the puddle. Regaining her composure, she vigorously wheeled smiling Pete off to get a change of underwear. Her uncharitable words trailed their rush to the toilet.

Sitting in a chair to Harry's right was Roxie. A sixty-something woman who always carried a cane, seemed always content, smiled at everyone, and nodded her head at appropriate as well as inappropriate times. One day a young pharmacy assistant arrived with supplies. While he waited for the nurse, Roxie sidled up to this friendly man who frequently made deliveries. Evidently, Roxie had been accustomed to chatting with him. Concentrating intently with his whole body, Harry barely understood the conversation. After small talk about the weather, Roxie glanced around the area. Seeing no staff in sight, she asked him if he would care to join her for "a little nip." The assistant said, "What do you mean, a little nip?"

"Not so loud," she whispered.

"You can't have alcohol in this place!" the naïve young man protested. She smiled coyly, took him by the arm, and ushered him to her room. Harry, now inquisitive, discreetly followed in his wheelchair. Once inside the doorway, she released his arm and unscrewed the crook of her cane. The assistant's eyebrows shot upward as she pulled out a small flask, took a sip, and offered to share with him. His face registered surprise and disbelief, and he beat a hasty retreat back to the safety of nurses' station, where he found protection in the company of the on-duty nurse.

Back at the nurses' station Harry looked at the several residents gathered near. All had either physical or mental limitations that labeled them as neither productive nor of benefit to society. Nothing was expected of them. They were sidelined just like he was. *A few months or so ago, my life was constructive and productive. I had my business, a house, a car and friends. I made good business decisions.* Harry mentally arranged his life much like a small child might arrange pretty marbles, and then he stopped short. *What about my business? This mental shuffle of thoughts and questions was maddening! If I could only talk with someone!*

Chapter Four

The Tucker men were interested in making money, and Harry had encouraged Tommy's interest in making money to pay for personal items and incidentals. There was no allowance in Harry's house when he was young. He told Tommy that he would appreciate money more if he had to work for it, and he provided him with chores, such as gardening, cleaning the garage, polishing shoes, or helping to keep the yard well groomed and tidy. These jobs were in addition to Tommy keeping his own room clean and sometimes washing dishes and vacuuming. Later Tommy got a newspaper route and sold vegetable and flower plants to his neighbors in the spring. In his teens Harry gave Tommy odd jobs around the laboratory in addition to his summer work of mowing lawns and miscellaneous paint jobs. His winter money-maker was the snow shovel.

As Tommy felt the power of generated earnings, he craved more and more. At age 12, he nearly had Harry convinced to allow him to buy a lot several streets to the west of their home with the $700 he had saved. It was a junky place, but Tommy planned to enlist the help of his friends to work for a day or two to clean up the vacant lot. Then he would paint a large "For Sale" sign and place it on the lot. He told Harry, "The lot will sell like cold lemonade on a hot day." Harry had liked Tommy's plan and pluck, but he had already invested money in several new pieces of equipment for his laboratory. Although keenly disappointed, Tommy planned other ventures. He dreamed of buying and selling numerous things that would make him a millionaire at a very young age.

He accelerated his high school studies and graduated in three years. Even during these busy teen years, Tom hired several of his friends to mow lawns for him. He kept busy repairing and painting fences. He also took on the job of painting a small house or garage. Toward the end of high school he mainly farmed out his jobs to his friends. Tommy majored in accounting/business in college and graduated at the top of his class, winning honors and some very good career opportunities.

Thomas chose to work in the advertising-promotion division of a major oil company that had several poorly managed convenience stores. One by one Thomas bought these unprofitable sites. In two years he had acquired six stores, and in six months they showed respectable profits. He now no longer needed the security of his regular employment. So he quit in order to manage his ventures full-time, devoting twelve hours a day to creating new ideas to feed his unquenchable appetite for business and making money.

When Thomas began searching for more profitable possibilities, he heard that his accountant was diagnosed with a terminal illness. He proposed to buy the accounting firm whose staff included two certified public accountants and three clerical employees. He began an aggressive advertising campaign, and this service soon required that he hire more bookkeepers. Once again his managerial and organizational skills had paid off.

Then Thomas dabbled in the new car business, but it was too slow to turn the quick profit that he was used to, so he went in search of more lucrative avenues. When Thomas was twenty-two, the local business association chose him as young Entrepreneur of the Year, a title he held for two successive years.

So Thomas was too busy to pay attention to either his father or sister. And, of course, there was no emotional bonding with his mother. His business had so consumed him that when he heard his father had suffered a debilitating stroke, he felt anger instead of empathy. He did not have time to attend to or support a crippled father. His unrestrained efforts in business had suppressed any feelings of compassion. In fact, Thomas took advantage of those who were sick physically or financially. Their bad luck was his good fortune. And now he wondered how he could gain control of his father's very successful medical corporation.

Harry lay flat on his back mulling over the facts. It had been eight or ten or maybe twelve months since his stroke. He had been getting both speech and physical therapy. Clara, his speech therapist, was of medium build and height with a well-formed mouth housing pretty teeth. Her long blond hair was usually gathered into a ` ponytail or French twist. He loved watching her lips overexaggerate to form words. She was married to a dentist and they had one small child. Harry had two sessions with Clara each week. Although learning to talk again was very frustrating, he really looked forward to their appointment. He was trying to form words she demonstrated, but all words came out sounding the same, "daa, aaa, gaa." His frustrations and discomfort manifested itself in outbreaks of various disagreeable emotions. Laughing at the crazy sounds his mouth emitted. Sadness. Tears. And sometimes utter discouragement.

Harry longed to share the burden of his affliction with someone emotionally close, but he could think of no one except his daughter, who was far away in a foreign country. He did not know if Thomas had contacted her, but judging from his present attitude and his rare visits to the rehabilitation facility, he rightly assumed his daughter was unaware of his calamity. Had Heather known, she would have immediately come to his aid.

One incident kept entering his mind, the first rung in his ladder of hope, or was it a dream or a nightmare? Sometimes it was hard to distinguish the difference. It happened one day during physical therapy. Kathy had attached the brace to his leg and ever so gently maneuvered him to a sitting position on the side of his therapy table. With open optimism flowing in her musical voice, she said, "Mr. Harry Tucker, the mysterious Mr. Harry Tucker, I'm really proud of the effort you have made to help yourself. Not many have such strong determination. I have felt your muscles becoming tighter and stronger. I detect the beginning of very slight resistance in your left extremities, which is a very good sign of awakening muscles. They're reacting positively, Harry! I think you are cooperating to the best of your ability. I believe, I have confidence, you will walk again all by yourself. You do your part and I feel that it won't be long, Harry, until you are independent again."

Like a flood of water bursting through a broken dam, Harry had felt a rush of excitement. A future? This was the first time in months anyone had actually given him any hope concerning a future. He looked away in an effort to hide his emotion. *If I could only thank her*, he thought. Better than talking, he would rather show his appreciation by some outward manifestation. *She probably thinks my sweaty palms are from this workout*. No. No! I had definitely not been dreaming.

Kathy could feel Harry looking at her. Her words had encouraged him, and his eyes spoke volumes. *Why can't the doctor or the nurse see his progress*, she wondered.

When Harry refocused on the exercises, Kathy continued her visual appraisal. *He's not that old, probably in his early to mid-forties. His athletic build is still recognizable. His always-a-bit-ruffled, brown, wavy hair gives him a rather boyish appearance. A square face, with wide full lips now puckered on one side. His jaw—he's determined. No; he's stubborn. I've seen that a time or two. His eyes are the darkest shade of brown I've ever seen. Sometimes they're soft, but sometimes they look deep within me. His nose is a little short but not too small, probably an errant gene from his European heritage. If his face didn't sag on one side, he would be quite handsome.*

Although Harry had aphasia, the inability to use words, he was making his own mental assessment. And it made him perspire all the more. Kathy's arm rested around his shoulders to support him, and he felt warm and comfortable in her embrace. He immediately recognized a long subdued emotion and jerked away as quickly as his deformed, ragged body could manage. Then he caught sight of her shoulder-length shining black hair surrounding a peaches and cream oval face. Her eyes were a brilliant blue, almost violet, so beautiful and yet warm, friendly and accepting … and innocent.

"Get a good grip on the cane, Harry." Kathy's voice brought him back to the task at hand. "We are going to strut down the corridor today."

She was always saying something of encouragement. Harry thought, *Boy, if I could just tell of my gratefulness to her!* He could feel that his good leg and arm were somewhat stronger, but the left side was as dead as petrified wood and nearly as stiff. If it were not for the fact he could see his left extremities he would not know they were still anatomically connected.

Kathy kept trying to motivate Harry. "You're doing fine. Your family will be proud of you. Just look at you! Put one foot in front of the other. That's all you have to do."

Had it not been for Kathy's physical support, his second attempt at stepping would have been utterly catastrophic. But on the third step, something happened that eventually helped dissipate his ever-present doubts. He was not sure if it was when he swung the affected leg or when his weight pressed down on that foot, but a shock wave ran from the tip of his toes into his hip and stopped in his affected shoulder. At the same time, there were prickly sensations throughout his entire paralyzed left side. "Aaahooooo!" he cried out. The cane went flying as he grabbed at his paralyzed shoulder.

Startled, Kathy gently but efficiently turned Harry around and nearly carried his entire weight as she rapidly headed for his room. She sat him on the side of his bed, swung him around, and laid him down. He was perspiring profusely and breathing hard. His eyes slowly closed.

"Heart attack!" Kathy screamed. "Yes! Now!" she shouted to the nurse, who was already on her way with a blood pressure cuff and stethoscope. "Blood pressure, 160 over 95. Pulse, 105. Respiration, 40," the nurse called out the stats. Another nurse rushed in with an electrocardiogram machine and soon reported: "The initial leads don't indicate a problem. His heart is beating rapidly, but it's regular!"

Harry glanced at those around him. *How stoic and resolute health care workers have to be*, he thought, looking at the set of their facial features. *But they're fast and efficient. Where is Kathy?*

Harry turned his head to the right and saw her. She appeared to be tense and apprehensive. Her eyes looked misty. Maybe she was allergic to the latex gloves she had hurriedly donned. The EKG nurse pulled the electrical plug, folded the cardiogram strip, and wheeled her machine out the door. Kathy leaned forward, put her hand on his head, and whispered something ever so softly. Then she disappeared. If she had looked closely, she would have seen a perplexed, yet pleased, expression on Harry's lop-sided face.

Harry ran a mental computer check on the experience. Yes, one person he had talked with once had experienced a similar sensation when convalescing from paralysis caused by a stroke. As he lay there, now recovered and breathing normally, he felt no sensation in the arm or leg that had tingled, no matter how much he stretched his imagination. The rest of the afternoon passed without incident. Yet Harry continually accessed his mental

24 — Escape from Bondage

computer to analyze the tingle and the whisper. He admitted to himself that he imagined both way beyond reality. But it was good to dream.

That evening after supper, Harry parked his wheelchair next to the nurses' station. During a pause of the usual nursing home sounds he heard singing. Not the off-key droning of the residents. He heard children! Children's voices were coming from the activities room. *How sweet are children's voices*, he thought.

Harry's mind scrolled back in time to when his Heather and Tommy were active in church programs. Harry had driven car-loads of children to shut-ins and nursing homes and hospitals to present various programs and Heather would frequently sing a solo. He loved to hear her sing. Her voice soothed his anxieties and quieted his nerves. *I miss Heather*, he thought, as he wheeled himself toward the sweet harmonies. *I wish she were here.* He rolled his chair toward the sound of the young voices and entered the room to see a group of a dozen or so boys and girls. They looked to be about seven to ten years old, with a few teenagers.

Harry focused on each child's face. *A clean-cut looking group of kids*, he thought. *What an angelic sound! I hope they know the strength and joy they are giving the residents!*

One tune after another was performed until a very pretty girl, about seven or eight, stepped forward and began singing, "Amazing grace, how sweet the sound …"!

The clear tone of the little girl's young voice was indeed sweet. He thought again of Heather. How he wished he could see her.

"… that saved a wretch like me!" the child sang.

That's one little girl who's far from being a wretch, Harry thought.

"I once was lost," she sang. The quiet of the room combined with the girl's sweet, innocent voice poured into an empty space deep within Harry.

"… but now I'm found." *I want to find life again, real life with a higher purpose. But first …*

"… was blind, but now I see." Harry glanced about, wondering if he was the only person so emotionally affected.

When the child finished, no one applauded. Some sat open-mouthed. Others' eyes stared intently at the little vocalist. Some with ancient wrinkles were smiling, or trying to. And all around the room, people were quietly shedding tears, while others fought to contain their emotions. All too soon the singing ceased. But the children began to mingle with residents; someone's mother, father, grandpa, or grandma.

The smiling children served cookies and punch to the residents, lingering a few moments to talk with each person, whether or not the person could respond. Most residents returned crooked, toothless grins. Harry was sitting on the sidelines, and so was Pete, whose obvious padding in his groin area indicated that he had been well-prepared for the occasion. The residents were having a wonderful break from the monotony and boredom of the quiet, all too quiet, life at the facility.

Harry felt a tap on his left arm. He turned and looked into the eyes of a child, the soloist. *She looks like Kathy!* He thought. When his surprise subsided, he realized she was holding his left hand.

"Hello," she said cheerily. "My name is Sari."

He wished he could return the squeeze of the soft little hand of the child with lovely sparkling violet eyes who searched his face. In his overwhelming desire to vocalize a response, he suddenly heard or felt something that sounded like, "Uh-lloo." Sari had already placed cookies and punch on the table within his reach and moved on to greet the next person. With a twinge of jealously, Harry watched Julia, old, crippled, and deaf, quickly reach out and hug the little girl. Overwrought with emotion, Harry wheeled himself out of the activities room to find a nursing assistant who could help him get into bed.

"It's a bit early for bed," she said as she gently granted his wish.

So many feelings stirred inside Harry after such a long time of emotional apathy. The heart-warming feelings caused by the presence of Kathy, his therapist, the sensations in his arm and leg, and the pretty little girl who reminded him of his Heather were all strong sentiments he had not experienced in a long time. Then there was the almost recognizable sound coming from his mouth. *Did I say a word, or was it just a sound coming from the noisy room?* he mused. Recalling the incident, he suddenly realized, that little girl had tapped him on his left arm. He had felt it! *Could it be? Really?* By this time he was thoroughly exhausted. It was hard to believe that he could have uttered a distinguishable sound or had actually felt the little girl's touch to his paralyzed arm. *My mind is playing tricks on me*, he decided as he drifted off to sleep.

Chapter Five

Many mornings later Harry was awakened by the voice of the hospital's head dietitian, Mrs. Bulwark. Although it had been a struggle over the past several weeks to get her to understand his dietary requests, she now was beginning to acknowledge the seriousness about the food he ate. He wanted the healthiest diet possible for he felt this was a key factor in his potential recovery. Harry was focused and tenacious about his ideas on diet. During her last visit, he had opened a Bible he had found in the nightstand and finally located the story about Daniel and his companions eating a simple diet of natural foods. With his good hand, he had rifled through page after page until Mrs. Bulwark impatiently retreated from his room, leaving Harry to his search. He spent a lot of time searching but finally found what he was looking for.

Harry had been dozing when Mrs. Bulwark returned an hour later, intending to quietly retrieve the menu selection form she had unintentionally left on his bed table. But Harry's eyes popped open, and having used his thumb as a bookmark, he was able to quickly open the Bible. He gestured for her to look to where he was pointing.

She was a little perturbed by his stubbornness, but he had already refused to eat for two meals. When Harry had first requested a special diet, Mrs. Bulwark thought that Harry's mind was as dysfunctional as his body. But after conferring with the doctor, she decided to humor him with the intent of re-issuing the regular fare of the day. Later on when much of the food was returned to the kitchen untouched, she began trying in earnest to create recipes that were nourishing and appealing to him. Still, some trays returned to the kitchen untouched.

Harry's insistence became a challenge for her to really try to please this man who seemed to know exactly what he wanted. Soon she noticed a healthy glow on Harry's face despite being confined indoors and despite his dietary quirks.

"How ah y'all doing, Harry? Is yo'ah tray of food ah'rot? Does it taste good to y'all?" She knew he could not respond by speaking, but his crooked smile spoke for him. Little did she know that his smile was not just for the concern she had for his diet. Mrs. Bulwark was cute in a rough sort of way, and he loved her drawl.

Now what did Harry want to show her? Mrs. Bulwark scanned her mind for clues. Then she read the sentence in the Bible where his finger rested.

"*Pulse*! Wot on uth is *pulse*? That's something yo'ah heart does, not somethin' yo'ah supposed to eat! Do y'all expect me to recreate something that's 5,000 yeahs old?" The determination in Harry's eyes overruled his shy, crooked smile. "Harry, you ah a caution, I de'clah! Wot am ah goin' to do with you!" Then she rushed off.

"*Pulse*! Wot in the wurld is *pulse*?" Back in her office Mrs. Bulwark leaned against the bookcase and let her eyes roam over book titles, hoping to quickly find the needed reference. She examined book after book, reference after reference. Then she conducted a thorough investigation of the dietary manuals. No luck. So she called Harry's doctor and asked, "Wot is *pulse*?" He answered, "normal is between 70 and 80. It's higher in children and lower in some older age groups."

Mrs. Bulwark was so embarrassed that she hung up without asking him anything else. She was too flustered to even say goodbye.

Next she called the American Dietetic Association, the dietitian at the Senior Citizens' Council in town, and the State Department of Human Resources. She got no answers but did get some sarcasm.

Then it dawned on Mrs. Bulwark. "Of cawse! It's a Jewish diet!" So she called not one but two synagogues in different cities. She learned that Daniel and his friends' diet of *pulse* was kosher, according to one rabbi, who rushed on to say that a kosher diet was the diet that God had given Adam and Eve at Creation. The other rabbi said *pulse* included some meat. "Such confusion!" she blurted, nervously running her fingers through her black hair.

Then Mrs. Bulwark remembered that Harry had the Bible opened to a section entitled Daniel. She went to the patient lounge, where she found a Bible and tried to nonchalantly spirit the book back to her office. Once there she immediately closed the door. She did not want to be seen reading the Holy Book, as she called it. Using the Bible as a reference and finding recipes from it was a new experience for her. What would her colleagues think if they saw her, a degreed professional, searching the Bible for dietary customs? *Not much more than they think of my drawl*, she told herself as she defiantly flipped the pages. However, she did not find the Daniel section, so she turned to the back of the book, where she discovered an index listing the books of both Daniel and Esther. Then she found examples of other Bible characters who had chosen a simple diet.

Finally she turned to the dictionary and found the definition of a food called "pulse": "The seeds of various plants of the pea family such as peas, beans, and lentils." Next she found encyclopedia references about *pulse* representing a vegetarian diet.

As Mrs. Bulwark compiled the information from all her resources, she was beginning to understand why Harry requested, demanded, that unusual selection of food.

"Wots a vegetarian diet according to Harry?" she wondered out loud. When she found him in his room sitting in his wheelchair with his eyes closed, she roused him, "Wot y'all call a 'pulse' diet, Harry? Why do y'all insist on it?"

Harry looked up, and a smile spread across his crooked lips as slowly as molasses on a cold morning. *Mrs. Bulwark is really trying now*, he thought. He motioned to the Bible still lying on the bed. She opened to the place in Daniel where she had first seen the word *pulse* in her own research. With his good hand Harry motioned for her to turn back to the very beginning of Daniel. She began reading the story of how Daniel and his companions had been enslaved. Yet these young people determined not to compromise their good health by eating the king's unhealthful delicacies or by drinking his alcoholic beverages. The man in charge of the slaves had never heard of the diet they requested, but he finally consented to give them a trial period. At the end of ten days, Daniel and his companions had better complexions and appeared stronger than the young men who had eaten the king's rich and refined food. Mrs. Bulwark closed the book, scowled at a smirking Harry, and stormed back to her office.

Harry also appreciated Elsa, the dietitian, because she took her responsibilities seriously. She neither gave anyone any "lip" nor took it from anyone. But beneath her frosty exterior, Elsa was warm and sincere. And now he discovered that she was reasonably flexible.

From his wheelchair, parked by the nurses' desk, Harry frequently observed the staff as they rushed about tending to the residents. He knew from personal experience how much was involved providing for patients' comfort. He also knew the staff could not take the place of family. Perhaps herein lay the problem that so many families, residents, and staff were encountering.

Harry witnessed visiting family members become provoked if they found their loved one wet or drooling or even when their bed was not made. They did not stop to think their loved one might very well have been in picture-perfect condition five minutes before their arrival. Harry had heard family members say, "He would be dry if he were at home." Staff members sometimes kindly encouraged the complainer to take their loved one home where they could have one-on-one care. The family's response was always the same. "It is more than I can handle, and I'm paying you to provide the needed care." Although the staff reasoned with them, "At home you are treating only one person. I have as many as fifteen persons to care for." Often the icy response was, "Hire more help!" But, of course, there was no budget to hire more staff. Harry concluded that the loudest and most angry families were feeling the most guilt about putting Mom or Dad into the nursing home.

A nursing home is no substitute for home, Harry thought for the hundredth time. He longed for his own home, for a visit, for comfort and support that only family can give.

Chapter Five

When he was able to think clearly about his hospital confinement, Harry focused on one bright light in his rather dark and dull existence, a student nurse named McGill. Every morning during the last several weeks, Nurse McGill would enter the room, greet each patient with a smile, and proceed with her work with a happiness and joy he could not forget. Hank, Harry's roommate, had suffered a bilateral stroke and so could neither make a sound nor move any part of his body. He had required total care for many months. Nurse McGill bustled about giving baths, changing sheets and pillowcases, singing or humming softly as she tidied up. She was an optimist. Her cup was always at least half full, not half empty. Harry felt better just having her in the room. Oh, how he wanted to express his appreciation!

But Nurse McGill had to transfer to another job to gain experience as part of her learning rotation. After completing her final task on her last day, Nurse McGill had put her hand on Hank's arm, looked him in the eyes, and said, "Hank, I'm going now, but I will remember you. May I say a little prayer for you before I go?" She talked to God about Hank's care and then left. Harry looked at Hank. His eyes that had neither focused nor appeared to comprehend for many months were now spilling tears. No amount of blinking or deep breathing could hold Harry's tears either. Nurse McGill was gone, but the fragrance of her caring, loving attitude would linger like cherry blossoms on the spring breeze.

His own emotions surfaced and gave him frustrated thoughts. *Where is Hank's family?* he wondered? *They should be the ones giving him comfort and encouragement.*

The next morning Harry awakened to the sound of voices surrounding his bed. Lying on his back, he did not open his eyes, but he was listening.

"Well, how is he doing, Dr. Cavendish?"

Thomas? Harry pressed his lips tightly to keep from trying to shout his son's name.

"Is he improving?" Thomas demanded. "Just what is the prognosis?" He brusquely fired off a number of questions without allowing the physician to answer.

Rushing in when Thomas took a breath, the nurse spoke, "Mr. Tucker is eating well. But he certainly has a different diet than most patients."

"I didn't ask about his diet!" Thomas thundered. Harry opened his eyes a fraction and through slitted eyelids he clearly saw the wing-tipped shoes of Thomas' attorney. To Harry's left and leaning against the bed was a woman dressed in street clothes. *Kathy!* Harry's very soul shouted. He struggled to remain silent and still. But from the train of the conversation, he surmised that Thomas and his attorney, Daggert, were trying to determine Harry's chances for recovery.

Dr. Cavendish finally got a word in. "With strokes we cannot predict the outcome. But more than likely, we have seen the major extent of your father's recovery."

Thomas noisily paced. He had a squeak in his shoe.

Harry knew that when Thomas frequently glanced at his watch as he was doing now, a signature move of his son, he was anxious to get on with the next hot business deal.

"What's the prognosis?" Thomas demanded. "What's going to become of him?"

Each time Kathy took a breath in a futile attempt to get a word in, Harry could feel the bed quiver as she tried to enter into the discussion.

"This is costing a bundle of money!" Thomas whined. "Is it going to pay off or not?"

He treats me as if I were one of his investments! Harry's heart cried out.

Harry could hear and feel the catch in Kathy's breathing after several unsuccessful attempts to be heard as Thomas raced ahead in his cold questions and heartless assessments about his invalid father.

This had only been Thomas' second visit. On his initial visit months earlier, he had found his father completely immobile, able to only respond with a semi-focused stare, unable to speak, unable to move, unable to acknowledge his son's presence.

Then Thomas ripped his father's heart in two. "He's no good to anyone anymore!" he bellowed.

Harry controlled his reeling emotions and demanded his body to remain still and his breath to flow quietly. Mustering his will, he quietly resigned himself to his own resources. He told himself, *If I survive this illness, it will be without any help from my only son.*

Harry longed to hear Kathy speak. Surely she would express some concern for him, but the evaluation had turned sour. His paralyzed hand was just centimeters from where Kathy's hip pressed against the bed rail. There was an opening in the conversation, and just as Kathy lurched into the conversation, the nurse interrupted. Harry tried rolling to his left side where his crippled arm was outstretched directly toward Kathy's hip. What he imagined to be a mighty heave was actually just enough to slightly brush against Kathy's backside. Her startled gasp did not attract the attention of anyone but Harry. She slowly turned around and with a surprised expression looked into Harry's bright eyes. She saw a slight shake of his head and read in his eyes that she was to be silent.

Harry could sense Kathy's ire building. Let her loose and Thomas would be no match for her. He would quickly feel like a penny asking for change. She crossed her arms and assumed a determined stance. Harry visualized Thomas' body language: boredom, stress, and impatience. If he had turned toward his father, he would have seen the recognition and pain in his father's eyes. But Thomas bolted through the door without a good-bye to his father or anyone else. Yet Harry understood quite clearly what Thomas barked at the doctor as he passed through the door: "Neither speech therapy, physical therapy, nor you have produced any appreciable changes! He is no good to anyone anymore!"

Soon the entire entourage was gone, including Kathy. The last expression he saw on her face was one of dissatisfaction. *I've made her angry*, he now worried. Later Harry would learn that her body language indicated surprise, disillusionment, and disappointment in Thomas, not Harry.

Chapter Five — 31

Thomas and his attorney were deep in conversation outside Harry's door.

"The only way I see it," Thomas was saying, "is to sell Dad's holdings and put him on welfare. We must put his assets into my name before this place takes them all."

Harry tried to relax his rock-hard, angry muscles and settle his whirling thoughts so he could evaluate their conversation.

"That will be a tricky affair," the attorney replied.

"That's what you get paid for!" Thomas' voice split the air.

"Look, Thomas," the attorney said, steering Thomas back into the room, closing the door, and spitting out his reply. "I could get sued for this negotiation. I would have to pay a huge fine! I could lose my license to practice law!"

Reading the coldness in Thomas' eyes, the attorney quickly shifted gears. Thomas paid exorbitantly for this kind of service, and the attorney wanted to keep that cash flowing. "I'll see what I can do," he said through clenched teeth, "but it will cost you." He whipped the door open and flew down the hall with Thomas hot on his heels.

Back at the nurse's desk, the doctor and nurses were discussing Harry's case.

"His vitals and progress notes indicate little change," the doctor said. "The notes record more optimism than realism."

"Dr. Cavendish," the nurse countered, "we have to report the facts."

"Yes, that is true. But with stroke victims, you never know. The longer they are in a coma, the longer the rehabilitation process, and the less chance for recovery. Harry's been getting speech therapy for weeks, and there is no indication of any progress. Physical therapy shows no increased use of his left leg and arm. I know Thomas. He does not want to put any more money into his father's rehabilitation," the doctor concluded.

After the doctor left, Kathy reviewed the charts, looking for new orders on her patients. All therapies for Harry had been discontinued. She was furious and disappointed. Her mental defense of Harry raged. *Can't the doctor see that his arm and leg muscles are getting stronger? I can feel resistance in Harry's muscles. His color is good. His attitude is generally satisfactory. It is true, however, he cannot speak and there is some question about his ability to hear. Didn't Harry communicate to me today? I understood what he did not want, didn't I?*

Then Kathy brought herself up short. *Is this some foolish notion I have? What's becoming of me? Besides, what was in Harry's mind when he indicated he did not want her to speak to the evaluation team? What makes me think I can read Harry's thoughts? A professional person is not supposed to get emotionally involved with her patients! And I am not! It's just that ... well, just that ... well, I'm not! But Harry has great potential to regain some degree of mobility.*

Kathy ended her internal monologue. But in quiet moments throughout the day, she questioned why she had so much interest in Harry. The doctor, nurses, and Thomas, whom she had seen in action, had all given up. *Unrehabilitable* constantly intruded into her thinking. She left the nurses station feeling that her efforts had been totally rebuked. It was personal, she finally admitted to herself. *I won't give up on any of my patients! No good therapist would.*

It was her unpleasant task to inform Harry of the change in his physical therapy program, and she dreaded doing it. She had to admit that she thought of Harry as more than a patient. *He is too young to be cast away like some piece of worn-out furniture.* Behind those eyes she saw more than the usual vacancy that many stroke victims demonstrated. She could sense a response from him. *Get a grip, Kathy!* she scolded herself. *You always get this way when doctors give up on patients. You know you can't restore them all.*

Kathy had always had a sense of when to quit with a patient and when not to. This was one of those times when she did not want to. Nor would she! That is, not if Harry would agree to cooperate with plans already forming in her seething mind. She could expect Harry's stubbornness to flare up, and perhaps he would see hers. But she would give him encouragement. He needed it. There was no one else.

Lunch was over and the halls were quiet as many of the residents rested. Kathy walked into Harry's room, pulled up a chair and sat down, leaning over just a bit to look closely at him. He opened wide his half-closed lids and flashed her that lop-sided smile that she had grown accustomed to. His eyes wandered. She followed their movement to their object of focus. They both stared; she with unbelief as a finger on his paralyzed hand moved. Both still staring a moment later, he moved it again. This time he made the motion for her to come closer. She leaned yet nearer and heard, "Hi." Her professional stoicism shattered into bits and pieces, completely unnerving her. She jumped up, leaned over, and without inhibition gave Harry the hug he tried not to wish for. Emotion surfaced on both of their faces, and it was several minutes before either could compose themselves. Snorts, sniffs, nose-blowing, and wet faces past, Kathy sprang into action. Now she knew for certain that the plans she was formulating only minutes before must now be activated.

Kathy blurted, "The doctor canceled all therapy, but he did not really know what he was doing. I must tell the nurse what has happened and get new orders written. I think your son wanted the doctor to think of other options for you because he is worried about all the money being spent. But, you see, it is paying off, and as soon as he knows about your returning ability to feel sensations and to communicate, he will want to continue and increase all therapies."

Kathy sure is fired up! Harry thought. He felt her excitement warming his heart. *She does not give up easily.*

Absence of visitors that Harry shared with fellow residents contributed to his increased feelings of abandonment.

Harry was acutely aware of medical protocol that after a reasonable length of time insurance mandated the discontinuation of therapies when a patient failed to show improvement. This time Harry was on the other side of the medical profession. He was receiving instead of giving, and he could now observe, perhaps become part of the provider to patient aspect of things. Yes, he knew medical protocol. This included, but was not necessarily limited to, a series of physical exams, diagnostic procedures, consultations, therapies, surgeries, treatments, and rehabilitation. The order and duration varied according to the diagnosis, insurance coverage, and cash.

Among most businesses and industries, there is the unspoken, age-old political philosophy, "You scratch my back; I'll scratch yours." Harry had been on a first-name basis with the majority of physicians in the area, had even played golf with several of them once a week. They and their families enjoyed free blood testing at his laboratory. He learned at the beginning of his confinement, some friends and office staff had sent flowers and cards. But people are not comfortable talking with someone who cannot respond in a conversation. They quickly give up and cover their conscience with the myth that the patient is unaware and doesn't know he has visitors.

Now was the time to have his back scratched, but everyone had disappeared. Even so, with his health care coverage and the small nest egg he had accumulated, there should be ample funding for any extended health need. Unless Thomas …

How thankful he was for Kathy. She gave him so much encouragement. She was still bursting with enthusiasm when she rushed to the door, turned, and said, "I'm going to call Thomas and tell him the wonderful news." She gave him a huge grin as she stepped towards the door. A slight back-and-forth head movement caught her attention. As she stared in amazement, she saw his lips form and heard a weak sound: "No."

She could not believe what she thought she had just witnessed. She didn't remember walking to his bedside, but she was there, staring at him as he shook his head from side to side: no. He could not utter any more words.

"But look what's happening! You spoke! You moved your hand! You are going to get well! I want to tell Thomas and the nurse and ask her to call the doctor. Everyone will be so happy!" she excitedly exclaimed.

He could not explain his motives. He had said only two, possibly three words in months. The excitement wrapped around his ever-present anxiety, and exhaustion shook him. The rush of emotions caused his lips to purse together, and his mind reeled. *I need time to think! I must think this through before allowing Kathy to report her observations.* Despite Kathy's insistent pleas, Harry rolled his head from side to side: no. Finally, exasperation and her need to attend to other patients pushed Kathy out of the room. Harry was left to sort out the events of the day.

Harry factored in that alarming sensation he had felt in his extremities days ago. He looked down at his paralyzed hand and tried to move his fingers again, but they did not respond. *Is my mind was playing tricks?* he asked himself again and again. Harry imagined a slight tingling in his foot. He cleared his throat, wanting to try to say something. Yet he feared failure. He summoned his courage and commanded his brain to encode the message. Silently his mouth formed letters. His breath rushed in to deliver the sounds. He whispered, "Thank You!" Tears rushed down his cheeks. He knew that people who suffer from a stroke or heart problems easily become emotional. Yet he found tears to be very frustrating even as a victory bath.

Just then a nurse entered. *Oh no! Did I not make it clear to Kathy that she was not to mention my breakthrough to anyone?* he asked himself. The nurse saw that he had been crying and just checked it off her mental list of usual experiences for stroke victims.

"I just came in to tell you that the doctor left new orders for you, Harry. He thinks you are doing fine, but he is going to stop the therapies for a while to give you a rest."

Rest? What does the doctor think I'm doing for twenty-three hours a day? Therapy only takes up one hour a day, Harry steamed inside.

Kathy continued to stress the positive. "The doctor thinks you have the best coloring of any of his patients. Must be that diet of yours, Harry. Maybe I'll try it myself. He thinks you should be up in your chair as much as possible. When you tire, Harry, we will lay you down. But do try to use the chair to get around. Go any place in the nursing home. In fact, go outside on nice days. The more exercise you get the better."

Harry continued fuming: *It's the only exercise I'll be getting from now on! I already go everyplace*, he thought to himself. The only place he avoided was the corridor with administrative offices. *That corridor … hmmm.*

Harry's stubbornness and self-determination was close to flash point. Yes. He had gotten over the anger about the stroke. Yes, he was accepting his lack of independence. *But I will not tolerate the underhanded way Tommy, my own flesh-and-blood-son, has given up on me! He has contrived with his attorney, Daggert, to take over my personal affairs and has denied the use of my own money to use for rehabilitation care and medication. He's preventing me from recovering! He doesn't love me. What has happened to Thomas? What am I going to do? I need to have help for aggressive physical activity, for physical therapy. But I have no way of contracting with or paying for exercise assistance. I have nothing! Thomas has my business. He is my Power of Attorney. He can do just about anything he wants. I have nothing except my name, which I cannot even utter. When I entered acute care, all insurance cards, credit cards, driver's license, everything in my wallet—and even my wallet—was taken from me!*

According to his children and friends, Harry had been the eternal optimist. Now his weakened mental capacity and the lack of support from the same people heightened his war against the barbs of negativity. The battle between optimism and negativity could go either way, but maybe his lifelong self-determination plus his stubbornness could produce a new and improved Harry. *I will be leaving this place! You can bet on it!* he promised himself.

Harry's anger powered his wheelchair at a higher rate of speed than normal. He was surprised by how quickly he arrived at the nurse's desk. He looked around at the other residents, and his anger overrode the panic he felt at possibly getting locked into living the non-productive life that so many of his fellow patients had accepted. *Not me! Not me! Not me!* The very idea agitated him until his blood boiled. As Harry's agitation increased, he felt the tingling sensation in his paralyzed side. *Got to take it easy*, he scolded himself, *cannot let my nerves get out of hand. Don't want another stroke. Take a deep breath, Harry, and calm down.* Hadn't he said these same words to countless patients? He breathed in deeply through his nose and pushed the air slowly through his lips.

As Harry began to feel a little better, he continued his observation. There was Pete being taken to the bathroom. Harry chuckled; now all Pete had to do was say "Beee" one time, and the nearest aide whisked him off, pronto. Sadie was pacing around, carrying the cane that concealed her happy-hour potion. Judging from their covert looks and their gentle teasing about her cane, Harry believed the staff knew that Sadie's hollow cane was never completely full or completely empty.

Then there is the patient, Harry Tucker, he considered. *I do have a mind and a determination. And normally I control my anger. Between one and a combination of these attitudes, we will see what happens. No one likes to talk with people who cannot return conversation. Maybe parents with young children would like that for a change, but not adults. Not me. People like me need live people around, people who talk and interact. I can listen. I can feel a handshake, a cool hand on my brow, a caress, a squeeze on the shoulder, and a slap on the back. I can understand if people would read to me; the newspaper would be good. What is happening in my community, or the world for that matter? I know what I need. Human contact from family and friends!* He determined when he was well he would form support groups to help others better understand how to physically and emotionally sustain stroke victims.

During the next several days, Harry found he could swing his impaired leg while sitting in the wheelchair. He could not get a lot of motion out of it, but when lying on his bed, he found he could pull the leg up ever so slightly and then extend it. He could roll his arm from side to side. When he was alone, Harry would repeatedly open and close his mouth for exercise. He was mouthing as many words as possible now, but never speaking out loud. This was a part of his plan, and he enjoyed thinking about his course of action. However this scenario might unfold, he determined to be discreet about it. This latest turn of events gave him stimuli. He thought of only one person with whom to share and discuss possibilities—one person who would be inclined to listen to Harry Tucker.

Chapter Six

Harry moved slowly, propelling his wheelchair through the corridors, pulling with his right foot and pushing the wheel with his right hand. This is what physical therapy had taught him to do, and he had quickly become proficient enough to get himself around the nursing home hallways. There were not many places to go, but he moved along the corridor observing the aides who scurried about their duties. They usually spoke to patients as if they did not expect a reply. The medicine nurse was passing pills but did not look up. Good! Harry was pleased that the nurses paid little attention to his frequent wanderings. Past the door leading to maintenance, past the rear entrance, and just ahead lay his objective. As he neared, he could already hear Kathy's familiar voice. As always, she was encouraging and coaxing her patient to exceed his or her comfort level.

Kathy had been stopping by his room occasionally to say hello and to give him advice on exercises he could do by himself. As he progressed, she gave additional guidance.

If he could have known what was going on inside Kathy's mind, he would have been wonderfully surprised and strongly motivated. Never had she treated one who stirred her emotions as did this man, Harry Tucker.

"Do not get emotionally involved with your patients," she could hear her instructors say. *But Harry Tucker's spirit has entered a soft place deep within me. Logic can argue against it, but my heart is putting up a good fight.* Yet Kathy gripped the reins of her emotions.

Kathy's primary joy was being at home with her son, Paul, and her daughter, Sari. Her husband, David, had found that being married tied him down and during the several years they were married, he found life outside the home to be more exciting. He slowly gave up all commitments and responsibilities to his wife and children. Kathy's heartaches, mental anguish, suffering, and pain ended in divorce. He had neither seen Kathy nor his children for years. Rumor had it he was a business executive on the other side of the country. She was still young and attractive and often noticed the opposite gender casting approving glances. She paid them no attention but kept her nose to the grindstone, for she was a busy mother with two children to raise. Kathy had determined that the torture she and her children had suffered would never be repeated.

Her children loved attending church because all their close friends were there. They were students in a parochial school, so Kathy had to carefully budget the one salary to support their household. Though finances were strained, they lived modestly and within their means.

Harry sat outside the physical therapy door, letting the sweet sound of her voice flow over him like dew on a rose. While deep in thought with his head resting in his cupped hand, the door opened and she came out with her patient. The situation startled them both, him because he was daydreaming and her because his visit was unexpected. Since his doctor cancelled treatments, Harry had not had occasion to visit the physical therapy department.

She dismissed her patient, wheeled Harry into the room, and closed the door. Looking around, he saw no other patients present and hoped this would be a good opportunity to try to verbally communicate. When he was alone and without fear of being overheard, he had practiced over and over, annunciating every word that came to his mind. They glanced at each other. While he admired her lovely violet-colored eyes, she softly giggled at his lop-sided smile. Much to her surprise, he opened the conversation by saying, "Hi!"

"Hello, Harry! Haven't seen much of you lately."

That sounded good.

"Keep up the good work. Practice talking with me anytime."

She could have stopped by his room anytime. But instead of worrying about that, he teased in a faltering voice: "Hel-lo Mi-siz- Car-son. H-o-w are we to-day?"

Kathy had joked about the way some nurses talk to their patients. He had practiced this greeting for days. His words were not clear, but she knew what he said. The sound of his deep voice awakened suppressed feelings within her. She forced them aside. This was the first time she had heard him speak a full sentence. She got up, scurried about the room, reorganizing and cleaning from her last patient's treatment and trying to appear composed but really needing a moment to mostly get a certain heart flutter under control. While she scuttled about preparing for her next patient, he noticed the grace and efficiency of her movements.

At last she returned, sat down again, and said, "Your ability to speak is returning, and I'm so excited! What a blessing! We need to broaden our plans."

Up close he saw the smoothness of her skin. She had a complexion that did not require powder or creams or whatever else many women think they have to wear. Her naturally long eyelashes enhanced already lovely eyes. He had observed that she did not allow her outward attractiveness to spoil the beauty within.

"I … h-h-ath … co-me for … ad-vith," he slurred and lisped.

"What kind of advice would you like?" she answered.

"Be-sides me, … no one … but … you … know what is … hap-pen-ing … to my body. How I am … getting stronger."

It was hard getting all the proper words in the right order. He knew he added a word here and there and had forgotten to say the proper word in other places and that his voice sounded like someone with tardive dyskinesia, a faltering speech. The words came out slowly, albeit not too clear, but her patience was encouraging.

She helped him with a few words, seeming to know how to draw out his thoughts. He was as nervous as a cat in a room full of dogs, but as he relaxed, his thoughts became better organized, and his words were easier to understand. He was soon able to fully express his ideas. He had a simple plan. He did not want anyone besides her to know of his progress. As far as what the doctor and nursing home staff would know, he was still paralyzed and speechless. None of the staff ever attempted to engage him in conversation anyway.

"Th-anks to you, I am slow-ly but surely re-hab-il-it-at-ing." This last word was more than a mouthful, but she understood.

He took a few deep breaths before continuing. "You … have … been my … streng-th, my sup-por-ter, my cheer-lead-er and now my con-fi-dante." He stumbled on some words and had to pause momentarily.

These were the most words he had spoken since talking with Tag O'Reilly eight or nine months earlier; maybe it was ten or twelve, he could not be sure.

Another long hesitation. "Will … you … keep … this … con-fi-den-tial?" Multi-syllable words gave him big problems.

"You put me in a predicament," she said." I have to chart all my patients' progress." Before she could mention anything else, he hastened on.

"Am … I … your pa-tient?"

"Well, technically no," she admitted.

"Does … the … doc-tor … write phys-ic-al ther-apy ord-ers in m-my chart?"

"No," she replied.

"Do … you … t-take … orders … from … m-my … chart?"

"No, you are not my patient anymore since Thom— … since therapy was discontinued," she answered cautiously.

"Do … you … ever … have … t-to refer … to … m-my … chart?"

Clearly, he had this situation well thought out. But he was now tiring.

"Harry, why am I getting the third degree!" she exclaimed with a chuckle. She followed his line of reasoning, knew where he was going with this, and decided his mind was becoming much more acute.

Softly, he continued. "I … have … been … thin-king a lot … about my … sit-ua-tion." He paused, in deep thought, and then said, "I am … tak-ing … too much … of your … t-time, I just real-ized. I am s-sor-ry. I am … so … in-con-sid-er-ate. I am … not … your … pa-tient." He struggled now to find and speak words. "I h-have … n-no … right … to … im-p-pose … on … you … l-like this."

He made motions to leave and started the wheelchair moving toward the door. She grabbed a wheel of his chair, steadied it, and faced him. "I am glad you are talking with me. You are an inspiration to me and I can make time for you."

She smiled. He relaxed.

"Talk to me," she encouraged.

Despite his distorted facial features, she saw frustrated emotions pass through his eyes and across his face. She knew how to empathize with her patients. With this one she sympathized. She felt his frustrations keenly. Never in all her professional career had she been met with such honesty and sincerity and now intense drive and persistence!

Over the weeks that followed, marked improvements occurred in Harry's ability to talk. His train of thought and his adeptness to speak allowed for sentences to flow longer and more clearly. Though her schedule was full, she found time for meeting with and listening to Harry as his plan unfolded. He seemed pensive today.

"Please don't think I'm feeling sorry for myself, although I have done plenty of that. I try to analyze my circum-stances re-a-lis-tic-ally and I value your counsel. I have been reduced to noth-ing, you know, thanks primarily to a dishonest attorney and an unloving son. In only a few months I have gone from a respon-sible tax-paying, law-abiding citizen, with a profit-able business and personal holdings to being a ward of the state, at the mercy of everyone else. I have been rejected and abandoned by family and friends and stripped of all identification. I don't even have clothes or shoes of my own."

Gesturing toward his shirt and pants, which were neither color- nor style-coordinated, socks and shoes, of like color but mismatched, he said, "These are from the laundry room. Left behind by some unlucky person. Either feet first or head first, doesn't matter; he's gone and I'm going too, but I'm going to walk out of here."

Her eyes moistened as he paused to rest and to catch his breath.

Taking advantage of this break, she leaned forward, placed a soft hand on his and said, "I know you have been deprived of many things. Would you consider having me as a friend?" My … my children also?" she stammered.

The unspoken message as their eyes locked was mutual. He momentarily lost his train of thought. It was hard to concentrate, so he simply said, "Thank you. I already do."

When he regained his composure, he continued, "I have always liked intrigue and challenge. Now I have both, the first a mystery, the latter a dare. When I have progressed sufficiently, I will leave this place. Intrigue will follow," he ended determinedly.

"Do keep me informed," she whispered.

"I will," he replied.

His primary goal was to convalesce. His second, a close runner-up, was to get out of the nursing home. That was the basic idea. Just how he would accomplish these objectives, he did not know. He would think on it. *Protocol! That's it! I must formulate a protocol. Actually two. One plan is for rehabilitating and another for exiting this place.* It had not entered his mind yet what he would do or where he could stay if or when he got out. He was focused on getting well and being independent.

It pleased him to think Kathy would be an accomplice. The momentum was building and he willed his body to get well.

She had entertained her own scenarios even before today's exchange. She would have bet on his complete rehabilitation long before Harry thought of it but she knew it did little good to push help on him; Harry had to want it himself.

Kathy, being a single mother and having a home to maintain, was very busy with full-time employment, which barely supported herself, her children, and paid the mortgage. There was cooking, washing, shopping, and a multitude of household duties to perform known to all mothers. The list of responsibilities was extended when single parenthood became her reality. She tried to make up for the children's lack of a father as best she could by camping, riding bikes, playing dolls with Sari, and playing ball with Paul. She had a first-hand conviction that all children definitely need a father to love them, not to mention the stability he would lend to the home.

Even though Harry's doctor had discontinued all physical therapy, Kathy knew she had the knowledge and ability to help Harry, and although she had precious little spare time, she was determined to adjust her schedule to support his progress.

When she came to visit him the next afternoon, he recognized determination on her face. Her expression turned professional as she announced, "I'm going to give you more exercises that you can do on your own. I believe your resolve and motivation to regain your health is strong enough that you will accomplish your desired goal with only occasional assistance from me."

She knew a little of the circumstances surrounding his family, but now that he could verbalize, she wanted to know more and he needed to practice talking.

"Do you have family who will help you?"

The sadness that crossed his face when he murmured, "No," did not escape her. "Will your wife be willing to spend some time with you?"

"No wife," he said simply. She knew that.

"Any other children besides your son who might help?"

He replied this time by merely shaking his head. She then asked a question, which, oddly enough, had been on his mind.

"How is your faith?"

He had recently been thinking about his Christian training of earlier years, how it had grown stale without his knowing it until it seemed that one day he woke up and God was not part of his life anymore. It really did not happen quite that simply or quickly. He had heard the call of the still, small voice but success of business and the busyness of life had dulled its sound.

"Are you a Christian?" she urged.

He was embarrassed to talk about it in her presence. He looked away.

"Only God can heal your body and mind. You have to have faith in Him."

Well, he knew that. Isn't that why he insisted on a better diet?

"God created our bodies and He knows how to repair them," she continued. Harry had similar thoughts.

"Do you want God to make you well again?" she inquired. He nodded, and while he was trying to put his thoughts into words, she took his hand and prayed. "Father in heaven, your friend Harry has suffered from a bad stroke as you well know. He wants to recover and we both ask You to help him. But Your will be done. Thank you."

With that she got up, gave him a big smile, and said she had to go get her children from school. He followed in his chair as she proceeded to the employee exit. She could feel his gaze on her as she departed. Passing through the exit, she looked back and, sure enough, he was still sitting in his chair outside her department door watching her. She paused, turned, and waved. To her astonishment, she saw he had his left hand slightly elevated and had managed to put up his index and middle fingers in the shape of a V, indicating the sign of victory. She smiled.

When she arrived to pick up her children, she was still thinking about this most extraordinary person and speculated about her plan of action for him. It was a little unusual for a patient in his physical condition to be so motivated. Her plans for therapy were interrupted by a child's voice she never got tired of hearing. "When can I see that nice man with the dark brown eyes at your nursing home, Mommy?" Sari asked.

"You mean Harry?"

"Is that his name?" Sari answered. "You knew just who I was talking about, didn't you?" Sari did not notice the slight tint that came to her mother's fair cheeks. Before launching into the details of her day's activities at school, she had one more comment, perhaps more for herself than her mom. As she busied herself preparing for the short trip home, she said, "I wish we could bring him home sometime. He looked as though he needs a friend, and I would like to be his friend," Sari added. Sari looked at her mom without further comment.

He now has two friends, Kathy thought.

All the way home, Sari was chattering like a disturbed mother squirrel about the day's events. Paul, as usual, was trying to get a word in but as was customary, he experienced extreme difficulty with "motor mouth" in full prime. Sari had some uncomplimentary comments for Paul as he kept interrupting, but soon they were happily relating mutual interests at school. Kathy looked at her children. How blessed she was with two happy, healthy, well-adjusted children in spite of the absence of their father. He had not communicated with them for years, and the children did not ask about him anymore. It was just as well, for Kathy did not know any more of his whereabouts than they did.

Sari was an outgoing child, an extrovert, who seemed to never meet a stranger. She was always helpful and cheerful. Paul was more reticent to meet people. He liked to read and had many of the usual twelve-year-old interests but mostly he enjoyed making "stuff." He saw usefulness in discarded materials and frequently brought home pieces of "junk," as Sari called it, much to his mother's dismay.

One Sunday Kathy went to the back yard, where Paul had spent most of the day. He had come into the house only once during the whole day with blackened face and greasy hands, and that was to eat. She approached his hammering and grunting and watched for a while to see what he was doing. He was so engrossed, she decided not to disturb him just yet and went back into the house. A couple of hours later, she went to the back door where Paul was calling for her. Her heart warmed as she took in the dirty face and broad smile.

"Come see my new invention, Mom." He reached out and took his mom's hand. He did not see her hesitate just a little as his grimy hand clasped hers. She did not want to diminish his obvious enthusiasm.

"You just gotta see our new clock."

"Clock," she said. "Do we need a new clock?"

Out behind the garage where Kathy had earlier seen him hard at his task, she saw his new invention and recognized at once what it was. Some of his inventions were not so easy to identify. "Just look at it, Mom. Ain't it a beauty?"

"Isn't it a beauty," she corrected.

"That's what I said Mom. A real beauty."

"Yes it is, Son. How does it work?"

It made him happy to have his mom interested in his projects. She always was, and now she showed more interest in this creation than with some of his other "inventions." She was always amazed at what this twelve (almost thirteen) year-old boy could do. He fixed just about all the mechanical and electrical failures around the house. He even installed a dishwasher once. Now here he was, smiling and telling her all about the clock. It was working too. He had gathered gears, belts, old bicycle wheels, and many assorted nondescript bits and pieces of discarded material, put them all together with bolts, screws, and had even welded a section or two here and there. He scrounged for a small electric motor and somehow had created a clock that worked. It was nothing for the mantel, however. But it was something Paul had accomplished with his own ingenuity and creativity.

"You have done a marvelous thing, my boy." Paul liked his Mom's approval and now her look of pleasure made him feel good.

"Know what I am going to make next, Mom?"

"No, I don't, Son. What will it be?"

"I don't know. Any ideas?"

"No, but I know you will come up with some wild scheme." The dirt and grime did not seem to matter on this boy she loved so much. She raked his disheveled hair, gave his dirty shoulders a hug, and went back into the house thanking the Lord again for such a wonderful gift.

Chapter Seven

Days and weeks passed on the calendar, although to Harry they seemed to drag on. He felt he was not making progress fast enough. As he lay in bed one night waiting for sleep to come, his heart filled with gratitude. He had been praying regularly now. After that pep talk from Kathy, the Holy Spirit convicted and impressed him anew to improve his relationship with his Creator. He was at peace knowing that whatever happened, he had assurance that the Lord, in His love, would not give him any problem too big to handle. He had heard that "man's extremity is God's opportunity." He thought to himself, *Why must a crisis occur before one calls upon the One in charge? Why would God want anyone to hit bottom?*

No identification—he could not prove his identity to anyone. No employment. No house, car, or personal belongings. Not even clothes or shoes. All he had for clothes were just leftover items from the Rehab center's laundry. Until a few weeks ago, he did not even know his name, let alone have the ability to say it. But God saw him, called him by name, and Harry was at peace. *Just show me the way, Lord, and I will try to follow You forever*, he prayed. *I trust that You know best.* He did have one other friend. He smiled at the pleasure that gave him.

A few mornings later Kathy stopped by his room to get a report on his progress. "How's it going?" she chirped. He raised his hand in caution and whispered, "When … can I come … to the … thera-py room?"

"Come just before quitting time, at four o'clock," she said. He was very careful not to let anyone but Kathy know of his accomplishments and particularly his speaking capability. A certain stubborn streak had kicked in, and he was determined to follow his plan. An incident recently took place that strengthened his resolve. The medicine nurse entered his room to give him his medication. He noticed a different-colored pill and refused to take it until she explained what it was. He still was not verbalizing, but she understood his reluctance. "The doctor has had to change your medicine," she explained. "Since your new, ah … ah, new insurance coverage began, you will be given this pill in place of the other medication." He now understood what was happening. He had wondered why the admission director changed the color of his name tag on the door to his room a few days ago. *Now I have a new insurance, a different medicine? I have been placed on welfare.* He nodded to himself. *That does it!* He seethed. *I'm definitely getting out of here one way or the other!* His long-range goal had just been shortened. He could not wait until the appointed time to talk with Kathy. He had been waiting outside her door for nearly an hour when it finally opened. The aide took her patient away and Harry rolled in. It was a breath of fresh air being with Kathy. She was always alert and smiling. He could not help but notice the fact that she seemed to take care of herself and take pride in her appearance. She closed the door and sat down.

"What's happening?" she asked. "Sounded like you wanted to talk about something. And do tell me of your progress. I'm sure the doctor and nurses would like to know of your improvements." She felt it prudent to not mention Thomas. "Your aphasia has improved and your diction and vocabulary have rebounded remarkably."

Harry thought he had noticed a difference in his facial muscles and his ability to speak also, but he did not want to become overly optimistic.

"I am still very weak and need to some-how streng-then my muscles, but instead of telling, may I show you how I am doing?" he asked, knowing full well she would consent. He proceeded to stand to his feet. Before sitting down, he showed her the range of motion in his left arm. He could bring his hand up to his face, could almost close his fingers into a tight ball and could say nearly all the words he chose to use in conversations.

"You … know … what they … have done … to me?" he exploded. Before she could answer his question, or comment, he went on, "they have … put me on … wel-fare! I am a total ward of the … state and-and I am being pre-scribed cheaper me-di-cines. Thomas has to-to-tally given up on me. I cannot believe he has … has stopped all fin-an-cial support." This outburst nearly exhausted him, probably more from the emotion of rejection by his family and friends than from physical strain.

"Calm yourself, my friend," she said with genuine gentleness. Trying to divert his frustration, she said, "What are you doing with yourself during the day? Are you going outside to get sunshine and fresh air?" She paused and then continued: "Remember the rules of health we went over the last time we talked? Let's go over them again just to refresh your memory." She had given him a bookmark that listed principles for good health. He had also researched little-acknowledged health principles spelled out in the Good Book.

"Number one, nutritious food. Is Elsa giving you good food?"

He nodded.

"What's the second one?" she quizzed.

"Exer-cise. I do as m-much as I can every day. And w-water is the third. I drink at least … eight g-glasses a day," he said.

"Now you should be working on the fourth, which is sunlight."

"I am," he said. "I go outside s-some-times sev-eral times a day."

She continued, "I think you have no problem with the fifth one; do you remember? Temperance, also known as self-control. Do you use tobacco, alcohol, or non-prescription drugs?"

"Of course not," he snorted. "I don't use caffeine either. It's bad for my car-dio-vas-cu-lar system." He thought for a moment. "And the next is fresh air," he volunteered.

"Number seven is getting enough rest. How are you doing in that department?" she asked. His slight scowl told her volumes.

"That's all I have to do," he retorted. But then the displeasure on his face turned into a look of contentment. "The last one has become a favorite, and that is trust in divine power." Harry had a peaceful countenance when he talked about his trust in the Lord. He had a renewed experience, and it showed. The change in Harry's patient status from private to welfare caused him to remember the recommitment he had made to entrust his future to God. Kathy saw his calm determination and reassured him that things would work out. He was very grateful for her effect on him. He had always been a little shy around pretty ladies, and this was no exception. As he glanced at her friendly eyes and warm smile, his anxiety was somewhat relieved.

"I have a surprise for you," she gleamed. "My children's school is planning another program in the activities room the day after tomorrow. Can you be there? By the way, what did you say to my daughter, Sari, the last time the school children were here? She often asks about you."

He chuckled. "It was a very intelligent conversation. I said something like 'uh-llo.' It was the first word I had spoken in months, and I wanted to thank her for the beautiful song she sang and to tell her how pretty she was, but the sounds my mouth made were pretty embarrassing and I'm not certain I actually spoke."

"Don't go spoiling my daughter with your blather," she teased. "You could easily win a girl over with that deep voice and those brown eyes."

She suddenly realized she had said too much, and her cheeks felt a tad of crimson rising. He noticed this but looked away and quickly changed the subject. He appreciated her staying past closing time, even though she did not seem to mind, but he promptly excused himself and waited outside her door while she tidied her room and locked the door. She gracefully walked through the exit door, but only after she turned, did she smile and nod good-bye.

Will Saturday ever come? he caught himself thinking. He wheeled himself outside the facility and headed toward the patio. It was a warm, sunny day with a pleasant breeze. He had been going out regularly for sunshine and fresh air.

He noticed a relationship developing lately between two residents, but no one else seemed to pay much attention. Mona had found herself a companion. It was interesting to watch them together. She, being in her eighties, and Jim, about the same age, did not seem to catch the notice of others as their friendship grew. They had probably been labeled senile, feebleminded, or as suffering from Alzheimer syndrome. Perhaps it was because Harry did not verbalize his responses that Jim confided in him about his feelings for Mona. Jim and Mona each needed companionship and had obviously found a satisfying bond between them. They ate in the dining room together and often sat wheel to wheel in their chairs holding hands. One day Harry overheard an aide chiding Mona about Big Jim.

Mona responded, "I'm probably being silly, but I kinda like him."

The aide encouraged her by saying, "Go for it! There is no reason you two cannot be good friends. I'll sing at your wedding," she teased.

The companionship did seem to increase their vitality. Mona began putting a little color on her cheeks and lips—a little askew some days when the lipstick did not hit its target, but Big Jim did not seem to mind. He began his days by splashing on a little cologne.

Chapter Eight

~~·~~ ❦ ~~·~~

Mona and Jim's relationship had not progressed to marriage status in either attitude or behavior. Theirs more accurately mirrored that of two teenagers' infatuation for each other. But the bond was strengthening. Out on the patio they were often observed with their heads close together, patting, touching and talking in very low tones and with broad smiles.

"Hi, Harry." Big Jim spoke while Mona sat quietly, smiling shyly. "I was hoping you were coming out here today. Come and sit with Mona and me. We want to get married! What do you think of that?"

Harry waved his hand and looked puzzled.

"Know why?" Big Jim went on, "Both Mona and I have family, but they never come to visit either of us and we are both real lonesome. We like bein' together. Her husband died many years ago as did my wife, and I, we, lo- … love each other," he blurted. Jim ended his speech in a sweat and Mona blushed. They both looked very satisfied with what he said.

Harry smiled, not quite so lop-sided, which neither one of them noticed, gave them a nod, a thumbs up, and wheeled himself to a secluded section of the patio so Mona and Big Jim could plan their future in private and where, undisturbed, he could practice a couple of steps to better health, more sun, and exercise.

Saturday afternoon finally arrived, and the residents were encouraged, so far as possible, to attend the children's program. Often groups came to either entertain with sacred or secular programs. Many residents were gathering today because this particular group had become special to them. These children were noted for their love and friendliness to all—even though some patients drooled, some waved arms with uncontrolled spasms, some groaned, some moaned, while others sat completely silent, totally incomprehensive of their surroundings. Maybe they could not speak, walk, or comprehend; that made little difference to these special children who regarded each resident with the same care, respect, and acceptance. As the children took their places, the room took on a semblance of quietness, and the leader took his position.

The sounds emitting from those young innocent faces were heavenly. They sang many of the elderly audience's well-loved old favorite hymns. One boy, about eleven years old, recited a poem. A girl then quoted the twenty-third Psalm. Too soon they were finished. Equally as enjoyable to the patients was the mingling afterwards by both sponsors and children. There's something about youth. When you're past it yourself, you want to associate with it as closely as possible.

Pete was beaming like a kid himself when a girl stepped up to him and began talking. She held his hand, looked into his eyes, and spoke to him as though he were the only person in the room. Sadie, holding her cane closely, which must have had a recent refill, was patting a young boy's blond head. Big Jim and Mona were enjoying the wonderful fellowship, too. They did not release each other's hand but were deeply engrossed in talking with a boy who said his name was Jim. Soon they became known as Big Jim and Little Jim.

The children were passing around punch and cookies, and Sari, with a shy boy in tow, brought refreshments to Harry.

"Hello, Mr. Harry." It was Sari staring at him when he turned his head.

"Hi. Who's this good-looking young man with you, Sari?" Harry asked in low tones. He was still trying to be discreet about his ability to verbalize.

She gave a nice sisterly smile as she said, "He's my brother. And his name is Paul. Don't tell him he's good-looking, it'll only go to his head, and I have an awful time living with him as it is."

Paul ducked his head and grinned. It was easy to tell he was not the talker his sister was.

"Did you like the program, Mr. Harry? Next time maybe I will play my trumpet," Sari declared.

Harry nodded his approval and was soaking up the attention given by the children when Kathy came up to their little group and laid a warm hand on his shoulder. *Why do I get goosebumps when she touches me*? he wondered.

"Glad you came to the recital. The children were all very excited to come, and especially this Sari girl of mine. She wanted to see you again."

"Can I tell him now, Mommy," Sari asked.

A pleased expression crossed Kathy's face as she said, "Yes, why don't you see what Mr. Tucker thinks of our idea?"

"You ask him."

"I think he would like to hear it from you."

Oh, oh, what plot are they conjuring up now, he wondered. Sari was still holding his hand. She squeezed it harder, looked into his face with those deep, deep blue, almost violet-colored eyes resembling her mom's and said, "I, we, Mom, Paul and I want you to come to our house."

Such kindness from people he hardly knew seemed too much. It took a lot of blinking and throat clearing before he could nod his head and softly say, "That would be nice … sometime."

He knew he would have to be in far better shape if he were to ever go house calling. The invitation had been made, and he saw the sincere look of expectation in their expressions. He smiled, squeezed her little hand, and realized he had a lot to be happy about.

The group of exuberant children eventually left. The room seemed to lose the cheerfulness the children had brought, and that old feeling of loneliness settled on the residents like fog on a lake.

Slowly making his way back to his room, he pondered many things. Harry was frustrated. He would like to go the Carson home, he thought, but he certainly could not go in his present condition. It was true that with the added exercises Kathy had given him he was getting stronger. It was still hard doing them by himself, but with this invitation, he determined to expand his workout schedule.

Next time I see Sari, I must thank her for the encouragement and the incentive she has given me.

He took the long way back to his room.

The nursing home was laid out in a square. Two sides of the square housed patient rooms, while the third side accommodated the kitchen, dining room, and laundry. The fourth wing included the facility entrance and contained business offices on both sides of the corridor, which were used only during the daytime by the office personnel. The lights were kept very dim at night because no one used this section when offices closed for the day. *Hmmm.* His thought process was picking up speed. An earlier thought just recurred. *This just might work*, he concluded.

Later that night when all the residents were in bed, the medicine nurse had passed her last pill, and the nursing assistants were relaxing behind the nurses' desk, Harry shuffled into his wheelchair, applied the leg brace, grabbed the cane, and left his room. He proceeded without incident to the long, darkened hallway and sat very still, thinking. He looked down the long, silent corridor, noticing the handrails, the pictures hanging on walls, the hard, tiled floor. Shivering at this last scene, he said to himself, "If I'm ever going to do it, it may as well be now."

He parked the chair close to a handrail, set the brakes, lifted the foot pedal, grabbed the handrail with his right hand, and sat wondering, worrying. *If I continue to sit here thinking about it, I'll never do it.* He finally heaved himself upright. Kerplunk!

He was momentarily stunned to think that this maneuver began and ended so soon. He was sitting. Luckily he fell into his chair. Visions of what the hard floor could do flashed in his mind. Before discouragement could raise its ugly head and take root, he heaved again. This time he swayed considerably, willed the dizziness under control, and then steadied. He felt light-headed, and tremors coursed through his weakened, hard-to-balance, crippled body. He was a fairly tall man, reaching a little more than six feet. The handrail was short for his height, but he found he could use it nevertheless. He slowly realized he had a death grip on the handrail and his hand would have to relax before he could move. He reached for the cane meant for his right hand but put it in his debilitated left. He thought now would be a good time for the exercises Kathy had tailored for his recovery. His hand felt comfortable in the grip of the cane handle. He wished his arm were stronger. He willed another ounce of confidence, prayed, and stepped forward.

He had not told Kathy of this venture, and now he wished she were here to guide him. Holding tightly to the handrail, he placed the cane forward about the length of his foot and swung his left leg forward. It landed beside the cane, exactly where he wanted. The sense of feeling was gradually returning to his paralyzed extremity, and he felt the pressure of his foot on the floor. He reached forward with the right hand and brought the right foot forward, leaning on the cane and braced leg. Once the right foot was securely placed on the floor, he swung the left foot forward, even with the right foot. He did it! Gaining confidence, he took another deep breath and tried again. Swing left foot forward, reach forward on the rail with the right hand, lean on left leg and cane. Now, bring the right foot up. *It's hot in here*, he thought, and then he realized it was because he was exerting himself that it felt so warm.

He went through the stepping procedure several more times before feeling exhausted. His legs felt as if they were made of noodles, cooked noodles. *I've got to sit down and rest*, he decided. He looked around for his wheelchair, but he was surprised to see just how far back it really was. He had not calculated this in his scheme.

Being analytical in nature, he reasoned he had one of two ways to get back to his chair. He could fall on the floor and crawl, or he could turn around and reverse the process. There was a big problem with the second option. Even if he could turn around, his right hand would be on the wrong side to hold the rail. With great reluctance, he considered a third method that entered his mind, he could try to go backwards, which would be more precarious and take a lot longer. But because of his growing weakness, he had to make up his mind—soon.

He decided to try the latter idea and braced his leg, stepped back with the right foot, brought the right hand back on the rail, and swung the left leg back. As hard as he concentrated on swinging the paralyzed leg backwards, it just would not go, so he ended up dragging it. After what seemed like an eternity, he felt the chair behind him. *Swoosh*. He collapsed into it, sweating great drops of perspiration and panting like a chased fawn. After fifteen minutes to a half-hour of reviewing his shaky performance in the darkened hallway, he felt encouraged. He actually had taken steps all by himself, the first of many, he resolved.

He rested for a few more minutes, then decided to try it again. This time his rhythm was a wee bit better but nothing to boast about, and it was oh-so tiring. This time he went a few more steps and then reversed. The backing up was fatiguing. He sat again for a twenty-minute break and then propelled himself upright. He was developing confidence and decided he would see what he could do by letting go of the handrail altogether. *Swing left leg forward, make sure it is well braced, and then use the cane with the right hand. Place weight on cane and step forward with the right foot.*

Accomplished! He was awash with sweat and not just from physical exertion. Now his thoughts turned to balancing without the aid of the handrail. He wished he had assistance while attempting this maneuver.

If Thomas had not taken everything from Harry and not made him a ward of the state, the insurance would have covered him and supplied the aid he so sorely needed. One step, now, another step. *Must not forget the rhythm.* He had no sooner thought that than he forgot it. He swung the left leg forward, and before waiting to set it firmly, stepped off with his right foot and fell on the floor; that hard, shiny floor that had given him chills earlier now gave him pains. Landing ungracefully but firmly on his posterior, with the left leg stretched out in front, the bulk of his weight was on his right knee that was bent under him. He sank completely to the floor, temporarily breathless and scared. There was a stabbing pain in his right knee.

Fracture, he immediately thought. He straightened himself out the best he could and lay gasping for breath. Now he was in trouble. He needed to call someone for help.

"Help!" he called softly, hoping no one would hear him and feeling sure no one would.

The sound of his voice gave him assurance that he could call for help if it were absolutely necessary. But if he did, it would definitely negatively impact his plan. He would get a tongue lashing from the aide, the nurse, the night supervisor, and then it would have to be reported to the day supervisor, to the director of nurses, and then to the doctor. No! He recoiled at the thought. They would then get an order to restrain him in bed and tie him in the wheelchair. *Must not risk it*, he thought.

He snaked his way over to the edge of the hallway where he could look up to see the handrail. *Got to pull myself up*, he said to himself. He reached up with his right hand and pulled. Not good enough. He pulled his painful right leg under him so he could sit on it. The pain caused him to be faint and dizzy. It nearly caused him to cry out. Tears came to his eyes. *Take a deep breathe and relax*, he calmed himself.

He had the presence of mind to release the leg brace locks. He took a few deep breaths, and this time, with a hand on the rail, he got himself onto his right knee. Now, upright on both knees, he was encouraged. Now up! He leaned over to lock the leg brace. Then he pushed his braced left leg out to the side and hunched to his right, pulling it as close in as he could, grabbed the rail with a death grip, and swung upward.

The loss of body weight over the past several months had paid off. He found himself up off the floor and leaning, sort of standing, but weaving unsteadily. He noticed his left hand was holding onto the rail. He was shaking like a leaf in the wind and perspiring so profusely that his hands were wet and slippery. His gown was thoroughly soaked. He mutely hoped it was all from perspiration, unlike Pete's soaked clothes.

Fortunately, the wheelchair was close by, and he inched toward it. Not stepping, but shuffling and dragging his left leg. The leg pain made him faint, dizzy, and nauseated. He sat in his chair for what seemed like hours. He then noticed the handrail had loosened and was sagging in the middle. A picture on the wall was noticeably uneven also. He could not remember hitting it. Maybe the flying cane had moved it. As he sat quietly, the dizziness gradually passed. The pain subsided somewhat but returned when he tried to pull himself along. He retrieved the cane laying in the middle of the floor and proceeded very slowly. He wheeled his way back to his room by using only his right hand to pull himself along the handrail.

"Where ya been, Harry?" his aide asked as he slowly approached his room. "I was looking for you. Don't tell me you were out visiting a lady friend."

Harry gave her a non-committal glance and went into his room. She followed and helped him into bed. He groaned inwardly, for the pain was intense. He settled down, tried to relax and before he knew it, fell fast asleep. Pain woke him several times during the night, but the satisfaction he felt and the exhaustion of his body lulled him right back to sleep after wiggling into a different position.

Chapter Nine

He slept late and did not rise when the breakfast announcement was made. He heard it, but thinking that this would be a good time to activate another part of his plan, he tried to go back to sleep. The aide reported his non-response to the nurse, who made appropriate notations in his chart.

By mid-morning he opened his eyes and lay very still, trying to separate the natural need to orient to the time of day with the emotions of a nightmare. The familiar hallway noises soon settled him. He remembered why he had slept in. It was because of his late-night, darkened-hallway affair. He moved his body slightly while mentally reviewing the occurrences of the night. He had gone to sleep worried that he may have injured his good leg.

If there was a fracture, it would not only be very difficult to explain but would also set him back weeks, probably months. He would have to learn to walk again with two bum legs. What an absolute horrible thought. He put his hand under the sheet and, as far as he could reach, palpated his legs. He found swelling and gross soreness in all the muscles. The closer to the right knee he rubbed, the more pain he found. It did not feel broken, but then one could have a non-displaced hairline fracture. He tried bending the leg. It hurt but was tolerable. He rolled it toward the inside and then to the outside. If it was indeed fractured, this maneuver, he well knew, would cause a lot of pain. He did not feel the pain a fracture causes and he was encouraged so he rang the call bell for help to get into his wheelchair.

Harry began his day with a ride along the hallway, not only to see what was happening but mostly to test his ability for the pulling process his leg would have to do in propelling the wheelchair. He found he could maneuver it with bearable discomfort. He was thankful there was no apparent break to the bone, but the muscles were very sore. He thanked the Lord for taking care of him. *He is indeed watching over me*, he thought.

He got a glimpse of Big Jim and Mona heading out to the patio, then he passed Pete, who waved frantically and gave him a one thumb up of warning … and, *look out! Crash!* The laundry cart, loaded so high that the attendant could not see where she was going, caught his wheelchair pedal holding his left foot and tumbled onto him. Sheets, pillowcases, blankets, wash cloths, towels, and the attendant herself were all over him as he lay sprawled on the floor. He struggled to pull free but could not.

Help was summoned and he was extricated from the rubble amid various exclamations of concern coming from all who had witnessed the accident. Even Pete was carrying on.

In the exam room, the nurse supervisor with two assistants laid him on the exam table.

"I know you can't talk, Harry, but can you point to where you are hurting?"

He did not respond, but he was very much aware of the examination. With his leg completely extended, she thumped him on his heel with her balled fist. *The hip is all right, or that movement would have radiated pain to the proximal femur*, he brooded. She proceeded to thrust fingers into sprained joints, grabbed super sore muscles, not so gently rolled his legs from side to side, and flexed and extended joints in his arms and legs. He winced. She apparently knew stroked people have a sense of pain and react to stimuli. He remained stoic throughout the entire examining process but had to close his eyes to hide the tears.

"Doesn't hurt, huh, Harry? You have minor abrasions on your legs, a scratch on the hand, and a knot on your forehead. There is a pressure spot across your bottom where you landed on your butt. Otherwise, you faired pretty well. We need to put a signal light at that intersection," she joked. To the aide she said, "Take him back to his room and monitor his pulse and blood pressure for the next twelve hours. Also, put him on complete bed rest." To Harry she said, "I believe there are no serious injuries but we will keep an eye on those sore places and have the doctor examine you when he comes in."

He lay in his bed gazing at the ceiling, recounting the incidents that had occurred during the last twenty-four hours. He thought of the program the children had presented, after which they had mingled with the residents, talking, laughing, exhibiting youthful vibrancy. What a breath of fresh air that was. Nice kids. Then there was the darkened-hallway adventure. It could have been a bad dream or a nightmare except for the pain that reminded him it was real. The pain gave him courage. Sometimes discomfort was a good sign. This morning's sleep-in and his missed breakfast would certainly alert Elsa. She would doubtlessly follow up by gracing his room with her presence sometime during the day.

"Hi. I heard of your accident," Kathy said.

He turned his sore neck toward the voice and saw his favorite physical therapist, a dream come true.

"Oh, you poor thing," she said coming closer and seeing what was now becoming a "shiner" in his left eye.

The kindness in her voice touched a tender spot in his heart.

"Are you hurting badly?"

Taking a minute to get control, he looked around to see who might be near. Seeing no one, he said, "lucky accident."

"What do you mean 'lucky' accident?" she hastily inquired.

"Between what happened last night and today's mishap, I am hurting." Oops, he let the secret slip. Last night's escapade was classified information.

"What? What happened last night? You had better start from the beginning, young man!"

He detected a gentle scolding in her voice. He could imagine Paul being reprimanded in the same tone. "How do I say this?" Honesty is the best policy and it was a life commandment of his. "You are finished working for the day, right? That means you're off duty?" She nodded in answer to both questions but had further interrogation in her expressive eyes. He continued before she could respond. "You don't have to report what I tell you because you are not asking as an employee, right?"

Her level of interest peaked. She nodded.

"Good!" he said. He knew he could trust her. "Last night I fell."

"You what?" She rested a firm hand on his arm.

"I applied the leg brace, slid into the wheelchair as you taught, and when the corridors were free of nurses and aides, I stealthfully made my way to the business office hallway where there is always subdued lighting at night, and decided to try to walk. No one uses that corridor at night and I thought I would likely not be discovered. I parked my chair close to the handrail, set the brakes, and stood up holding the rail with one hand and clutching the cane with the other." He did not mention his enormous feeling of insecurity or his great desire to have had her with him. "I did very well until my leg gave way and I fell. I crawled back to the chair and nursed my aching body and wounded pride. So you see the laundry cart accident with the resulting trauma covered last night's injuries." He paused, took some deep breaths and continued, "My legs hurt from last night's fall. The injuries on my arms and head were caused by the laundry wagon collision." She saw the area around his eye was darkening. He forged on. "I was really worried the fall may have caused serious injury to my legs, but I was even more concerned by the probing, twisting, and turning the nurse subjected me to during her painful examination, which included not only the head and arms, but the legs also. She said I seemed all right but would ask the doctor to examine me on his next visit."

The professional therapist in her suddenly took over and she ran her expert hands over all the sore spots he mentioned plus other bruised areas of which he was not aware until now. He maintained silence when Kathy asked about other painful or sore spots preferring to keep his bottom out of the picture for now.

"Does this hurt?" she repeatedly asked as she pressed against sore spots.

He could mask some reactions to her pressing and prodding. She placed her hand gently on his cheek to turn his head slightly toward her. When she leaned down to take a closer look at his bruised head, he got the closest look yet into her eyes. If she had been listening to his heartbeat, she would have called a cardiologist to report a case of cardiac tachycardia or irregular heart rhythm.

When she finished her examination, she concurred. "Probably the nurse is right. There seem to be no broken bones or serious injuries except for some superficial abrasions, a blackening eye, and several small hematomas, but we don't know about structural damage without X-rays. I'll urge the doctor to order some. I'll suggest he order radiographic examinations of both knees and lower legs, probably the hips too," she added as an afterthought.

"Miss Kathy," he sometimes called her this in an effort to avert familiarity, "Miss Kathy, I'm already feeling better," he fibbed. This was the mere skin of the truth. He winced. "Please talk with me before you talk with him."

"But you could have a permanently damaging injury," she pleaded. He insisted. She glanced at her watch and realized she was already late picking up her children from school. With a word of caution for him to stay in bed, she excused herself.

The next morning Harry awoke to aches and pains throughout his entire body. It felt as if he had been run over by all the residents and their wheelchairs. He forced himself to a sitting position and moved closer to the edge of the bed where he could dangle his legs. It took effort to move them, but he moved them slowly, first forward, extending the knee, and then backward, then from side to side.

I can tolerate this, he thought. Now just the good leg. *Which one is that?* he queried. After the fall, both were hurting. He gave the right leg a good talking to and then moved it farther forward, slowly letting it fall back. After a minute of this, he moved the good foot behind the left and proceeded to push it forward and then let it slowly move back. It was torture, but he focused on his goal. Fifteen minutes of this and he was ready to rest.

An hour later the usual hallway noise startled him awake. It was still a while before lunch and he desired to get out of his room. Laboriously, he swung to the bedside, applied the leg brace, and literally fell into his parked wheelchair. Pedaling himself along, he found that using his leg and arm was excruciatingly painful. He sidled up to the handrail with his wheelchair and pulled himself along using only his hand. *Let the leg rest*, he thought. It was slow going because other residents were parked alongside at various intervals.

He went completely around all four corridors using his leg only when necessary. He stopped when he got to the infamous area where his accident occurred and surveyed the damage.

The handrail was dangling precariously, and he overheard office employees speculating as to how it happened. After listening a few moments, he smiled knowing none of their theories were correct and proceeded onward.

As he was passing physical therapy on his second trip around the corridors, Harry heard Kathy's voice as she worked with a patient. Just then the door opened, and Kathy, surprised at seeing Harry up, asked why he was out of bed. He did not verbally respond because they were in the presence of others. She noticed pain on his face but fierce determination in his eyes.

"I'll talk with you later, Harry!"

Was that an impatient tone in her voice? He returned to his room to see if he had received any mail, all the while knowing he had none. It was a nice thought, though. He had entertained the thought of filling out and sending in postage-free information cards found in magazines just so he would have some connection with the outside world, even if it was nothing more than junk mail.

Kathy's "later" was toward mid-afternoon when a cancellation gave her time to go look for him. Harry was not in his room. She looked on the patio, where she saw Big Jim and Mona, but there was no sign of Harry. Jim and Mona had not seen him all day, they said. Of course, that was no surprise since they had eyes only for each other. She looked in all the places he normally hung out. On a whim she decided to look in the chapel.

There he was in his wheelchair toward the front of the sanctuary, head bowed and resting in both hands. She came up behind him very quietly and dropped into a seat beside him. He raised his head at the gentle swish of her arrival.

"Nice to see you," he said, and meant it.

She detected a marked improvement in his speaking and significant reduction in his facial lopsidedness. It was not nearly as noticeable these days. She smiled, and again he noted the full mouth with straight teeth, her peaches-and-cream complexion and rose-petal lips. He wanted to reach out and touch her smooth cheek.

"I've been searching all over for you," she whispered, respecting the sanctity of the chapel. "I looked in your room, out on the patio, in the dining room, all over. I was afraid I'd lost you."

Harry wished there was more truth to that than just a figure of speech.

"Hard to get lost in this place. If someday you do not find me in the building, please do not worry," he added.

"Either I was overly concerned about your injuries or you did not hear a thing I said," she added. He appreciated her protective concern.

"Miss Kathy, I am in a great deal of pain," he confessed, "but I had to get out of bed and move about to prevent more stiffening of my arms and legs. Besides, you confirmed the nurses' opinion that nothing was fractured and I trust you more."

His confidence warmed her. "I felt compelled to come in here." He continued, "There are so many things for which I am grateful and here is where I find great peace."

She knew there was more he wanted to say so remained quiet. He turned to look at her as best as he could with his very sore body and then shared a very personal and private feeling that he had been wanting to express for several weeks.

"Of the many things for which I am thankful, you top the list."

She lowered her eyes. She knew he meant it.

"You saw me as no other professional or unprofessional person did during my extreme illness. It seems you have taken a personal interest in my progress, but then I notice this same caring, encouraging attitude demonstrated to all your patients. I am aware that your help has gone way above the usual call of duty, and I am indebted to you. I have nothing to give you in return except my prayers, and that is what I was doing when you came in."

Kathy felt good sitting beside Harry and knowing he now trusted in divine leadership for his life. What he said raised curious emotions within her. Just as she opened her mouth to respond, someone came in, and she noticed her break time was over. As she arose, she gave his shoulder a gentle squeeze. He would have winced because of the soreness but he loved her touch even through the pain.

He turned his chair around and accompanied her into the hallway, saying, "Maybe I will go to the patio, though it is sometimes a little embarrassing to sit there on the patio with Jim and Mona because … well, they just seem so happy and I do not want to disturb them. They have not shared their joy with everyone just yet."

"I think true happiness should be shared," she spoke in thought. "It does look as though they are developing a genuine love relationship. Their constant togetherness is no secret around this place. The fact is, Harry, secrets are not kept long here."

He shot her a perplexed glance with questioning eyes. "Oh, you do not have to worry about your covert activities or your improving condition," she hastily added. "You are no longer officially my patient, remember? So I do not have to report on you anymore." She gave him a heart-melting smile. "Besides I gave you my word, didn't I?"

He immediately felt ashamed.

"Sorry," he said. "I came into the chapel for more than one reason. I shared the first with you. The Christian programs the children have been giving along with their talks have helped me rethink my priorities. I have come to understand God's love for me. Even if I never walk or become productive again, I want God to have first place in my life. He knows what is best for me, and I trust Him with the remainder of my life."

He did not see the mist that came to her eyes as he continued to affirm his commitment to the Lord. When he finally looked at her, he saw only deep concern and Christian love, and he knew it was for him.

"I am very happy for you," she said as she turned, then she excused herself to go back to work.

At the door she looked back and stated emphatically, "You are pretty awesome yourself," and she was gone.

Every time she left him, Harry felt a little empty but was thankful for the peace he had found with his Maker as well as his friendship with Kathy.

Chapter Ten

The activities director did a good job in providing informal functions. There was bingo, puzzles, passing balloons from resident to resident, spelling games, and, for those who were able, occasional visits to the shopping mall. But time passed so slowly for some of the residents. That was Harry's experience.

One day after lunch as he rested, he pondered his quest to regain his mobility. His injuries were healing nicely. In fact, when the doctor came for his regular visit with patients, Harry's name was evidently not on the list, because he was not directed to go to the examining room.

He knew the only way now to regain strength as soon as possible was to walk, exercise, and eat nourishing foods including plenty of fresh fruits and vegetables. This would ensure he would be on his way to better health. The traumatic experience of the week before was still vivid in his mind, for his sore body was a constant reminder. He probably should tell someone of his late-night jaunts, but he wanted to hide them for as long as possible.

He made his way to the patio and slowly continued to the far end of the building, where he had never been before. The area was paved and his wheelchair rolled easily. He practiced pulling with his right leg; then he attempted with the left one. By now he could wiggle the leg a little. He took the foot pedal off the wheelchair and let it fall to the ground. He mentally reviewed the procedure: *lift the foot, swing it forward, and when the heel hits something solid, pull forward.* At first there was more grunting and groaning than movement. Gradually, as he strained his leg muscles, the wheels moved ever so slightly. After an hour or more of struggling, he was actually pulling himself along with the left leg. By this time he was really tired, but he smiled with satisfaction.

As he rounded the corner, a loud voice startled him: "What are you doing out here?"

He jerked his head up and saw Larry, the maintenance man. "Admiring your beautiful flowers," he said without thinking. "Larry, you startled me."

He had noticed how beautiful the flowers looked viewing them from inside the window. He caught himself and did not say more. Larry did not seem to have much contact with the nurses, but still Harry must be discreet.

"Be careful," Larry warned as Harry replaced the wheelchair pedal and went back inside. He was anxious for the night shift to come on duty. Eleven-thirty was late, but he slept in late every morning, so at this time of night he felt wide awake. He cautiously perused the hallway. There was still too much activity. He would wait another thirty minutes and check again. Finally, as some resident's clock struck twelve midnight, all was relatively quiet, except Old Man Clark. His yelling attracted the attention of the nurse and aides, so now was a good time to scoot around the corner and charge toward his objective.

Soon he was around two corners and in the darkened hallway. He was still sore from having fallen on the floor and from the laundry cart collision the previous week, but he had checked his injuries daily and they seemed to be healing well.

He was standing in position now, supported by the handrail in one hand and the cane in the other. He was ready. *Remember the procedure. Grip handrail with right hand ... and cane with the left. Lean into rail towards right and reach forward with the cane. Now bring left leg forward even with cane and right foot.* The first step was agonizingly painful. *Rest a minute.*

OK, let's do it again, he encouraged himself. Right hand on rail, move cane forward, lean into rail, and swing left leg forward, even with cane and right foot. *Not bad*, he thought. For the first ten minutes he held tightly to the rail because of the distracting discomfort. Then he rested in his chair. Bones, muscles and tendons that were already weak from paralysis and inactivity were traumatized by the fall and the laundry cart accident. But they were favorably responding nevertheless.

While resting for a minute, he thought about the simple exercises Kathy had taught him to do on his own; pulling and stretching maneuvers he had done in bed at the beginning of his rehab. He was sure they had helped in regaining and maintaining strength as well as making the joints and extremities more flexible. Still, he felt weak and thought he would benefit by more advanced exercises.

Enough rest. Up! Get a secure grip on the handrail, he ordered. *Do the same thing again.* And he did. He spent more time resting than standing and walking. He did not care. He had actually walked! All by himself, too! His confidence was building. *Pride goes before a fall*, he cautioned and sat thinking. Many thoughts passed through his mind. Thoughts of Thomas' attitude. How he had denied restorative programs. How he had given up on his own father. Thoughts of being given up for a "nobody" were bad enough, but the abandonment of friends and those he held in high regard was devastating.

He wanted to proceed one more time and started to rise, but his legs felt like rubber, soft rubber. Through an open office door he glanced out a window and saw what he thought was the early light of dawn. *I must get back to my room and into bed before the shift changes and early-arriving employees start milling around*, he thought.

He went to the darkened hallway every night now and slept-in every morning, refraining from responding to the morning nursing assistant's calls and concerns. He usually did not awaken until nearly lunchtime.

One morning Thomas entered his father's room and spoke to him. No response. He spoke again, this time louder. Harry was zonked out. Worn out from the previous night's workout. Or at least that is the way it appeared. He heard Thomas say to the nurse. "Mr. Tucker seems to be asleep, or else he is comatose."

"Yes," the nurse answered. "You know, when a person has had a stroke, he sometimes sleeps a lot, and we have noticed recently that your dad is developing a pattern where he does not awaken until about noontime each day. There has been no other noticeable change. Perhaps you could make your visits in the afternoon. He seems to be wide awake then and moves about in his wheelchair."

"How is he doing otherwise?" Thomas inquired.

"He eats well," she answered, "and his vital signs are within normal range, and generally when he is awake, he reacts quite normally for a person with his medical history."

"Thank you," Thomas grunted and made haste for his office.

Days passed during which Harry was up practicing late into the night and into the early morning. One night while going through his routine, he suddenly stopped when he heard an unusual sound. As he looked down the long, darkened hallway, rounding the distant corner and heading straight toward him was the night nursing supervisor.

I'm found out now, he thought to himself. Fortunately, he was at that particular moment resting in his wheelchair. With only a slight pause, he swung around and very quietly headed in the opposite direction. He made silent haste as he rounded the nearest corner. She had her head down, and if she saw anyone in the darkened hallway, she evidently assumed it was an employee. As he turned and peeked back around the corner, he saw her enter one the offices. In a moment she came out with a folder in hand, locked the door, and headed back in the same direction from which she had come.

"That was a close one," he whispered to himself. He wiped his brow, waited until the pattering of the nurses' shoes and the thumping in his chest subsided, and proceeded with his workout.

One day several weeks later as he was talking with Kathy, he suddenly realized he was stronger. She, too, noticed his strengthening physique.

"It must be from a healthy diet and all the exercises and walking the hallway," he told her. They both agreed.

He could even hold on to the rail with his left hand now and felt fairly comfortable doing it. It was still weak, but strength and dexterity were returning. He was concerned about being over-enthusiastic and tried to temper his relentlessness, but the desire to escape his situation and environment, coupled with the sense of being a ward of the state, mercilessly drove him.

Night after night he doggedly persisted. Day after day he slept late. He could now leave his cane in the wheelchair, and when resting from walking, he would continue standing, grab the handrail with both hands, and do knee bends. While resting and catching his breath, he would never be completely still, first bending and swinging one leg and then the other. He tried doing anything he could think of to get the circulation moving, to gain muscle strength, and improve balance and coordination. He was succeeding, although he wanted to do more. He wished he knew of rehabilitation exercises that were specifically designed to restore strength for a patient with a stroke, but that was currently being denied him. Kathy told him of exercises he could do, but that was not the same as being shown and assisted. Being alone like this presented an element of silent danger that was always haunting him. He knew that when a person had a stroke, the heart could be affected. It could be weakened. He had to force himself to slow down.

During the weekend Sari was thinking of Harry. She and her friends were praying for residents of the nursing home, and his name in particular came to mind. Every Saturday in church her whole class participated in asking God to be with him and to allow healing.

One Sunday evening while they were doing the dishes and cleaning up after the evening meal, Kathy observed her daughter deep in thought. Kathy could tell when she had something serious on her mind, for she had a habit of chewing on her lip , raising her right eyebrow and humming a nonsensical tune. "What are you thinking about, dear?" her mother asked.

"Huh? Oh nothing. Just ruminating." Sari liked big words.

"My, that's a really big word. What are you cogitating about?"

"What does that mean, Mother?"

"The same as ruminating."

"I can see you are thinking, ruminating, or cogitating about something very serious," she said with a smile.

"Oh, it's not all that serious. I was just thinking of poor Mr. Tucker. He must be very lonesome all by himself in the nursing home. None of his family ever comes to visit. I was comparing my life to his. I am always happy or should be, thanks to you, Mommy. You make sure I have nourishing food, a nice place to live, plenty of friends, clothes, and lots of love. It just does not seem right for me to be so happy while Mr. Tucker is all by himself. I feel so sorry for him," she almost wailed.

"I know, Sari, I think of him and so many other residents who seem to be dumped in the nursing home and left to strangers' care. I know of some who never see friends or family except at Christmastime. And even then, they do not have a visit on the holiday, but either before or after. So many of them would love to go to their family's home anytime and especially on holidays, but they rarely ever do. And I will tell you something else, many times a son or daughter will move into their parents' house after they have placed their own Mom and Dad in the nursing home and then never invite Mom or Dad back to the house they rightfully own. They must have feelings of guilt about that. Then there are those patients who have not had a visit from family or friends for years."

She abruptly stopped talking.

"Sorry, Sari, I did not mean to criticize. Sometimes circumstances prevent patients from returning home. There are those who outlive family and friends, grow old, and cannot get out to visit anymore. For these reasons I am thankful for the nursing home and for the dedicated people who work there. I am also grateful for your school's willingness to visit the elderly. You can see how the residents love to hold on to you. You remind them of what they once were. You children are a real comfort and encouragement to them."

Sari thought about this. She had a habit of raising one eyebrow just slightly when in serious thought.

"In school we are reading about some groups of people in this country who would never think of putting their parents in a nursing home. They make room in their own home, often giving them the best rooms in the house. Isn't this what it means to honor your father and mother, Mommy?"

"You are right about that, dear," Kathy replied. Just then the back door opened and closed with a bang as Paul entered.

"Gross! Go to the bathroom and clean up!" directed Sari. "Your unmitigated appearance reminds me of a pig! Have you been wading in a pigpen?"

Paul came up to Sari and pretended he was going to smear her face with his dirty, greasy hands as he said, "Whoa! Some big words for a small fry."

"Leave me alone, Grimy," she cried. Paul laughed. He enjoyed teasing his sister.

"Whatcha talkin' about? You both look like the cat ate our favorite canary." Mind telling me so I can solve the problem?" he smiled through his dirty face.

"We don't have a bird," she said and shot him a disgruntled look. "We were just talking about all the lonely people at the nursing home. I would like to do something for poor Mr. Tucker. I know you like him too."

"Let's bring him to our house." Paul was the practical one. No sense stewing about something. Just do it!

"Oh, could we, Mommy?" Sari asked. I know he would love to come and I'll take care of him. I know you are sometimes very tired, but Paul and I will care for him, won't we Paul?" Once an idea was in her head, she persisted.

"Hold on just a minute. The fact is I have been thinking about that also. Maybe if you both agree, we could invite him … sometime … I am just wondering … . She did not finish because nice thoughts were running through her mind. A slight flush came to her cheeks that the children did not see. They did, however, notice the pleased look on their mom's face whenever Harry's name was mentioned. Tonight was no exception.

"Please, Mommy," both kids chimed in unison.

"Yes, I think it is a good idea. How about I bring him with me when I leave work tomorrow. I'll put him and his wheelchair in the van, pick you up from school, and we will all pitch in to prepare the best home-cooked meal he has ever had."

"Yeah!" they both chorused, and the plan was set.

"We do have to get permission from the facility. But I think I know how to do that. We will bring him home for the evening and I will promise to return him by nine o'clock."

The children did not hear the entirety of their mom's last comment. Sari was making plans for Harry while Paul was on his way to the shower devising some of his own.

The next day just before lunch, Kathy found Harry in his room, still in bed, in fact. "It's lunchtime. Are you going to the dining room?" she asked.

He yawned, smiled in mock surprise, and said, "Is it that time already? What do you suppose is making me sleep so late?"

She shot him an all-knowing glance. "Yes, it is late, but I know why you are still in bed. I have something to ask you," she said, ignoring his sly smile.

"That will be different. I'm usually the one asking you for favors," he grinned. He was such a good-natured fellow, she thought.

"Sari and Paul want you to come for supper … and I do too," she hastily added. "We all want you to come today. I've got everything arranged. I must go now because I am late for my first morning's appointment," she said as she darted out of his room and headed to her department. She feared he would protest, so she did not acknowledge his call as she turned and left. She knew she would have a visitor in the physical therapy room very soon.

All grogginess left Harry's head in a hurry. He immediately thought of multiple reasons why he could not go. Good reasons! He had not mingled with outside society for well over a year, and he had no street clothes because Thomas had taken them from him, thinking he would never have use for them again. He probably had already given them to Goodwill or thrown them away.

Chapter Eleven

Harry was up quickly and, not stopping to comb his hair, got into his chair and began pedaling fast.

"Whoa! What's the rush, Harry?" the nurse asked as she dodged him coming around the corner. He gave her a hurried smile, still not saying a word, of course, and propelled himself onward.

"Harry, they are waiting on you in the dining room. Your lunch is already on the table," she spoke to his back. He grunted. *Blast it! I've got to talk with Kathy, but I had better eat lunch first. I am hungry and she will still be working after lunch.*

By the time the meal was finished he had calmed considerably but was still very apprehensive about leaving the nursing home. He threaded his way through the dining room traffic and maneuvered himself to physical therapy. This time he was too impatient to wait until Kathy dismissed her patient. He knocked. Moments passed, then the door opened and Kathy stuck her head out smiling.

"Yes?" she said.

"I can't go," Harry whispered.

"Why not?" she whispered back.

"Well, I do not have a thing to wear," he said with a woman-type dilemma. "Well, there are many reasons," he moaned.

She smiled again, revealing a natural genuineness, and said with mischief in her eyes, "Now you sound like a woman. Don't worry. I have thought of everything. Your aide will get you ready. Meet me by the back exit at four o'clock. Do not get to stewing like an old grandmother."

With a twinkle in her eyes, she closed the door and thusly left him with a moderate to severe case of panic and a host of concerns. *Good thing there is an activity going on this afternoon*, he thought, *or else my nerves might get the best of me.* In truth, he really wanted some time with Kathy, for he wanted to demonstrate what he considered to be a physical therapy marvel.

As arranged, he was waiting by the employee exit at four o'clock when Kathy came out. "I'll bring the van around," she smiled. Getting Harry into the van was a lot easier than she had thought. She noticed he had gained a lot of strength and body coordination and did most of the movements by himself. But she did not have time to tell him how good he was doing because he needed to discuss his apprehension.

"I'm really nervous about this, you know. It has been more than a year since I have carried on an intelligent conversation for any length of time."

"Thanks," she said sarcastically with a smile.

"I think you know what I mean," he corrected.

Being far enough away from others, he could now speak freely. His eyes were intent on his surroundings as they drove along. He was hungry for the outside world.

While he perused his surroundings, his eyes moved from side to side as though he wanted to take a mental picture of everything. He visually consumed the environment.

Kathy wanted him to see all he could and so took her time driving to the school where Paul and Sari were waiting. They arrived all too soon, and the children packed into the van, both chattering.

"Slow down, children. We have all evening and you will have plenty of time to talk with Mr. Tucker."

Just that morning on their way to school she had explained to the kids that Harry might act a little slow or maybe show some signs of apprehension as a result of his stroke and because of his lack of opportunity to socialize. The children had often talked with their mom about a variety of medical conditions, so they were knowledgeable of and sensitive to handicapped people. Nevertheless, Kathy did not want Harry to feel embarrassed about his clothes or his impairment or to be stressed in any way.

True to form, Sari was the first to speak, almost sitting on Harry's lap. She had her arm draped over his shoulder when she looked into his face and said, "I'm glad you are coming to our house today."

As he turned to look at her, he again took note of her eyes, which were like her mother's—blue, so dark blue they were almost violet. Sari always looked at the person she was talking to. That was a sign of honesty, he thought. His heart warmed at her acceptance. Paul was a little more reserved, but perhaps that was because Sari had a way of monopolizing a conversation.

"I want to show you my inventions, Mr. Tucker," Paul finally inserted when Sari took a breath to re-energize for the next barrage.

"You kids will have time for everything," Kathy said, trying to take the intensity off Harry. They arrived home and Kathy said, "Wait just a minute and I will get your chair out."

Before she got to Harry's side of the van, he had the door open and was standing with only the aid of his cane. Kathy gasped in surprise, and both kids stood staring. He took a step or two while they just stood and watched.

"Surprised?" he looked at Kathy, who was approaching him now. She took his hand and pummeled him with questions and exclamations.

"What are you doing? Be careful! Watch out! Don't fall! Wait! I'll get your chair!"

"Mom, one thing at a time. We'll have all evening to ask him questions," Paul chortled.

They had a good laugh, but Kathy insisted Harry ride in the wheelchair as they entered the house, saying, "I knew you were progressing very well, but I had no idea to this extent." While Kathy and Sari prepared supper, Paul sneaked Harry into the back yard, where both fellows enjoyed themselves looking over Paul's tools and his "inventions."

Harry recalled his own childhood days when his dad gave him free reign of his equipment and tools to encourage his creativity. He examined Paul's clock and could not repress a smile. It was amazing what he had learned to do with such a limited inventory of tools and equipment.

"Looks real good, Paul." He allowed Paul to explain the movements, but he was curious to know where all the parts were found.

Paul could not remember but shrugged, "A little here and a little there, I guess."

"Paul, do you have Harry out there?" Kathy called from the back door.

"Yes, Mother, we're just coming in."

"Now you must not wear out Mr. Tucker before he gets to eat. Remember, he has been very ill and is still recovering."

Kathy was not scolding because she really enjoyed a man taking an interest in her son's projects. She tried very hard to show interest in his creativity, but it takes a man to understand a man, she nodded.

Harry elegantly held Sari's chair while she took her seat, much to her enjoyment. When they were all seated, Kathy nodded to Paul, and he offered a short but fervent prayer of thanks for the food.

Supper was superb!

"Tell me how you made the mashed potatoes, Sari," asked Harry.

He had noticed she was whipping them when he and Paul entered through the back door. It took very little prompting to get Sari talking.

"Well, Mr. Tucker, first you peel the potatoes."

"Everybody knows you have to do that, silly," said Paul.

Unperturbed, Sari continued. "After you boil them, you put them in a bowl and whip them. Add a little milk, a little melted margarine, and then add some finely chopped garlic and a little salt. Do you like them this way?"

"They are absolutely scrumptious," he said. "A gastronomical delight."

Unbeknown to Harry, the family was vegetarian, therefore, the entire fare was totally compatible with his diet of "pulse."

When he noticed the absence of meat on the table, he asked, "Have you ever eaten flesh foods like beef, poultry, or fish?"

"Don't even know what it tastes like," Paul stated.

"Yuck! Who could eat blood?" Sari added.

Kathy moderated the tone of conversation as she said, "I am thankful people may eat the way they choose; that's the freedom God has given us. But He has also given His created beings guidelines, which I try to follow. The way I understand it, He wants the best for us and has provided everything we need in fruits, nuts, vegetables, legumes, and grains."

"Everything! Even Brussels sprouts and cauliflower, right, Sari?"

Paul enjoyed goading her.

"I suppose you think He gives you chocolate chip cookies," Sari shot back.

"No. You make those for me because you love me," he teased.

"Oh, you!" she exclaimed and then smiled.

A lot of love in this family, Harry thought to himself. *Kathy has done a good job with her children.*

When the meal was over, he and Kathy made their way to the living room while Paul and Sari washed the dishes. He noted that neither one grumbled about the task of doing dishes and cleaning up after supper. There was pleasant chatter from the kitchen while the two adults sat in the living room.

"Thank you!" he said and meant it, looking at her. He noticed, not for the first time, her smooth, porcelain skin, her startling clear blue, almost violet colored eyes, the oval face, wide mouth with full rosy lips, and shiny black hair. Outside her working environment she seemed very relaxed as she sat across from him and smiled, knowing he was looking at her. She knew of many men who appraised her and most for the wrong reason, but she did not feel uncomfortable with Harry. In fact, she was doing her own survey. She saw that his going outdoors to get fresh air and sunshine and to exercise had tanned him. There was now only a slight indication of drooped facial muscles. She saw a broad forehead, rich brown eyes, a small nose, wide lips, and a pugnacious chin that dimpled in the center. He had also filled out in muscle and strength. He now sat erect, not with hunched shoulders or with the look of despair of just a few months ago. There was now a natural confidence and determination about his pleasant features.

"You're getting well and stronger by the day, and you don't look anything like when I first met you. You are looking the picture of health and vitality. You could do for some new clothes, however."

They both enjoyed a laugh over his clothes, which helped alleviate his embarrassment. His own clothes had been taken from him at the time of admission to the rehabilitation hospital before transferring to the nursing home, so he only had the dressing gowns provided by the home.

Kathy had talked with the laundry lady knowing there was always some unclaimed clothing. They had found a pair of brown pants, which were too short, and a pastel yellow shirt that was missing a button. Harry was thankful for them, however, because he had envisioned going on his first visit in a patient gown. He appreciated her thoughtfulness. She had assured him she had taken care of everything, and she had done so.

"You certainly surprised me when you practically jumped out of the van and started walking without assistance. Tell me exactly what's been happening. You are going faster than I can track you."

"Well," he began, "as you can see, I have gained a lot of strength in both legs and arms. My fingers are a little stiff, but I can grasp and hold things. When I look in the mirror, it looks like my facial muscles have firmed up. There are a couple of places in my leg that are numb, but it does not seem to be significant, at least when it pertains to mobility. My walking coordination needs to improve and I have a limp, so my cane is a constant companion. I eat and drink without assistance. All this adds up to quite a bit of progress, don't you think?"

Kathy nodded in agreement and said, "You have done remarkably well to achieve that much. Most people have daily rehabilitation therapies with professional assistance. Now look at you—you have done it all by yourself. You've done all the work, with no one to aid you."

He lowered his eyes and his face took on a soft expression as he said, "I must thank you for the encouragement and support you have given me. I was so far down I had to look up to see bottom. I felt abandoned by my family and was ready to give up when you talked with me one day. I still recall what you said. Do you remember?"

"Yes, I remember. I can see you in my mind's eye now. You were downcast, could not speak, and had no control of body functions. You were a pitiful sight. But you had a determination that I rarely see and then only in people with more to start with than you. I said to you, 'You can do it, Harry. I can see you walking, talking, and back at productive living soon, but you will have to work hard to do it.'"

"That's right, and that little talk gave me the spark of encouragement I needed. It was that and two other things; one having my faith in God renewed, for which I'm thankful to you, although actually it was you and your daughter, Sari."

"And what was the other?" she asked.

"It was—" Before he was able to say more, Paul and Sari burst into the room full of enthusiasm.

"My, but I don't see where they get all that energy," exclaimed Kathy." "Your visit with us this evening has given them a spark of excitement. Let me rephrase that, your visit has given both the children and me a spark of enthusiasm."

The children soon had Harry and Kathy in a game of Uno. One game led to another, and before they realized it, the grandmother clock in the living room struck nine. With a flurry of activity, they hustled out of the house, into the van, and were back at the nursing home just a few minutes late.

"If they don't like me being late, maybe they will kick me out," he joked.

He was feeling good.

"Don't get in trouble," Sari said. "We want you to come again." And without waiting for a response, she continued, "Don't we, Mommy?"

But before Mom could answer, Paul said, "We sure do."

"That makes it unanimous. We want to give you an open invitation to come anytime" continued Paul. "Right Mom?"

Harry's eyes grew misty when he said, "I can't remember when I have had a better evening. Certainly not since my own children were your ages."

The children stayed in the car while Kathy wheeled him to his room. As they were about to leave the car, Harry turned and spoke to Paul, "I have an idea for an invention for you, actually for me, but one for you to devise. I need to give it more thought before I give you the basics."

"What is it?" Paul asked anxiously.

"I'm still formulating the concept in my mind, but get in touch with me sometime this week and we'll talk about it," he suggested.

Two days later Paul rode his bicycle to visit Harry right after school dismissed for the day and eagerly searched for him. He was not in his room. Paul felt proud that Harry showed an interest in his mechanical creations and felt even better that he trusted him to fabricate something just for him. His heart swelled at the thought he and Harry were kindred spirits. Paul found Harry in the chapel.

"Hi," they both spoke at the same time. He wheeled himself outside the door, and Paul opened the topic right away.

"What is the idea you want me to work on, Mr. Tucker?"

"Call me Harry, if you don't mind."

"My mom will have my skin if she hears me calling you by your first name."

"That's OK. I'll talk to her about it."

They talked at length about Harry's idea. Paul was only twelve, nearly thirteen, he interjected when his age was mentioned, but he had a good mental picture of Harry's concept before they were finished talking. The older man found Paul to be very perceptive, and by explaining what he wanted to achieve, Harry encouraged the young man to let his creative juices flow.

For the next several days while Paul was fabricating, Harry was exercising. He really needed some better method of exercise to help improve endurance, strength, and muscle tone, and he hoped Paul's device would be what he needed.

He was up late every night and some nights until the early morning hours. Then Harry would surreptitiously return to his room, climb into bed, and sleep late. The schedule was more taxing on him than he wanted to admit. He knew his body had been weakened by so many weeks and months of debilitation.

For the first several weeks following his stroke he had not eaten by mouth. His nourishment was administered intravenously and through a naso-gastric tube. He had lost thirty pounds, as was evidenced in body strength, muscle size, and tone. Rejection by his family and friends had a profound influence on his psyche. It was by sheer willpower, a renewed confidence in God, a moderate, healthy diet, and Kathy's encouragement that had propelled him thus far.

Lately, though, he was experiencing periods of weakness, shortness of breath, and occasionally slight dizziness. Upon returning to his room from his workout, convinced it was only fatigue, he would crawl into bed and immediately sink into a deep sleep.

Chapter Twelve

～⌒♋ ♋⌒～

One night after his darkened-hallway dynamics, Harry crawled into bed, went to sleep and was suddenly awakened by a smothering sensation. He took several deep breaths, realized he was perspiring, and felt he could not get enough air to breathe. He pulled the string of his call bell, and soon an aide entered. She laid her hand on his arm and was about to say something but changed her mind quickly. She reached over and pulled the call bell from the wall.

He could hear the loud non-stop dinging the detached call bell made at the nurse's station. The registered nurse on duty came puffing in, expertly put her finger on his neck pulse, saw his labored breathing, and felt the clammy skin, turned to the aide, and ordered, "Get oxygen immediately and send in the electrocardiogram machine."

There were muted murmurings among the nurses while an oxygen tube was adjusted for nasal administration and the cardiogram was recorded. The head nurse viewed the strip and headed out the door motioning for the others to follow. Outside the door their voices were subdued, crisp, and businesslike. The evening supervisor entered, visually ascertained that protocol was established, and then exited.

Five minutes later a paramedic and an emergency medical technician entered his room and took over. One viewed the cardiogram strip while the other took his blood pressure and other vitals.

"Pulse 65, respiration 25, BP 96 over 40," he voiced. "What did you get, nurse?" asked the paramedic. These were the first audible words Harry could understand since this episode began. Everyone was speaking in whispers, nods, and knowing glances. He was unceremoniously loaded onto the ambulance stretcher and quickly removed from his room. They paused at the nurses' station and picked up some papers as the nurse said, "Take him to Memorial Hospital and hurry."

Harry was justifiably concerned. He understood the protocol, was aware of the need for tests and their results, but still he was annoyed by the reactions of the medical personnel. *They think because I do not talk, I do not comprehend either.*

Inside the ambulance the paramedic was on the radio talking with medical personnel at Memorial Hospital. Harry listened to the one-sided conversation. "BP 98 over 46, pulse 68, respiration 30. All vitals stable. Roger. Oxygen increased to 6. One ml. epinephrine, standing by. Sending EKG strip. Roger." The paramedic finally looked into Harry's eyes, smiled, and said, "I think you are going to be all right."

Wow! he thought. *If someone had only said that sooner, whether or not it was true, I certainly would have liked that assurance.* He silently whispered a prayer of thanks whereupon he took a deep breath and tried to relax.

With red lights flashing and sirens wailing, they entered the emergency patient area at the back of the hospital. The siren's mournful cry gradually subsided and became silent but not before Harry was quickly removed from the vehicle and rushed to the trauma room. Within seconds from the time the ambulance doors opened, he was in a very active emergency room. He noticed crash carts, large multi-drawer tool chests on wheels stocked with emergency use drugs and materials, an electrocardiogram machine and several people standing by. A portable x-ray machine and a host of other equipment were visible.

Mark, the paramedic, was briefing the nurse on the en route vitals including the last requested order for 4.5 liters of administered oxygen. "Anyone know this guy's name?" someone shouted through the doorway.

"Yeah, he's another one from the nursing home," an attendant shouted back.

I wonder what that means, "another one." Might as well have a number, he thought.

"Records indicate he stroked out twelve months ago, right-sided CVA, complete paralysis on left side, does not talk," finished the EMT.

The usual procedures included blood tests, electrocardiogram (another one), oxygen, and a chest X-ray. These and other tests were done almost simultaneously. *An efficient team*, he thought.

"Keep him here for a while and someone stay with him!"

Must be the doctor talking.

"Looks like he'll be OK. Do BP every thirty minutes until the tests come back," he instructed and left the room. "And somebody stay with him," he repeated.

After everyone left, the LPN straightened up the room, pulled up a stool, sat down, and put her hand on his arm. If people only knew how comforting it is to be touched by a caring person. To feel the warmth radiating from a concerned pat, a genuine smile, or an expression of acceptance is the assurance a patient needs.

He glanced at her nametag, which identified her as Jeannie. She took his blood pressure again, recorded it, and sat back on the stool.

"I think I have seen you before somewhere," she said. "Have you ever seen me?"

"I heard them say you cannot speak, Mr. Tucker, but if you understand my talking, nod or shake your head.

He dipped his chin slightly while looking directly into her eyes.

"Ho! We can communicate," she cheerily noted and began asking only yes and no questions.

"Do you have pain?" He moved his head to one side.

"I take that as a no?" He nodded slightly.

"Good! Do you have discomfort anywhere?"

He nodded. She stood, looked alarmed, and said, "Where?"

His lips curled slightly at the edges as he placed his right hand over his bladder.

"Oh, I see," she said smilingly and promptly produced a urinal. He indicated he could assist himself and after placing the urinal under the sheet, she backed out, closing the curtains behind her saying, "I'll return in a minute."

Some things take longer than a minute, he thought. She had to stay close for continuous monitoring so stood just outside the curtain, humming.

When she reentered, she did another blood pressure and commented on his tan.

"Where did you get such a nice tan? Hard to get one like that in a nursing home."

She looked into his questioning eyes and asked, "Are you scared?"

Interesting, he thought. *She is sensitive, knows how to cut through barriers and get right to the point. I like that.*

He raised his shoulder just a tad and she responded, "A little, huh? Well, the doctor says he thinks there was no serious damage if this was a heart attack but we need to wait for the results of all those tests we have done. Your blood pressure is normal, as well as your pulse and respiration. You'll be chasing those nursing home ladies before you know it, she grinned." She was so nice he could not help but return her friendly smile.

Later the triage nurse rushed in waving a sheath of papers and said, "Mr. Tucker, the report of your tests are nearly all normal, but the doctor wants you to stay overnight and get some more blood tests in the morning. Will you do that for us?" she asked, nodding. Without waiting for him to answer, she said to Jeannie, "Please take Mr. Tucker to room 314."

She left and they headed for the third floor. As they waited for the elevator, Jeannie moved to the side of the gurney and asked, "Do you have family to contact? Your chart indicates only to call the nursing home in the event of an emergency. I'd be happy to make the call for you," she smiled with a look of concern.

He diverted his eyes to the side and she looked sad. He was put into bed, a final blood pressure was taken, he was wished good night, and was left to rest.

Where have I seen Jeannie? Her face and personality haunted him. He could not remember that she had ever worked for him, nor could he recall her as one of the many burned out nurses at the nursing home. *That personableness ... hmmm.* Light suddenly dawned. *That's it!"* he exclaimed to himself. *"She's a friend of Heather's."*

She used to come to Harry's house to hang out with his daughter. They were friends. He made a mental note to tell Heather, if he ever saw her, that her friend is a practicing nurse, and a good one, too.

It was hard to go to sleep with all the activity and excitement that comes with being a new admission. However, sometime before morning he must have dozed off, because as light flickered behind his eyelids his fuzzy brain and filmy eyes recognized familiar sounds coming from the corridor.

Patients were being taken to early morning appointments. Mop buckets, medicine carts and food wagons clanged in the hallway. After an institutional breakfast of canned orange juice, canned grapefruit slices, Jell-O and a cup of coffee, which he did not drink, a resident physician entered and emphatically stated, "Mr. Tucker, you are a lucky man! The symptoms you presented on your emergency room exam initially indicated your heart was giving you a little trouble. We did all the usual blood tests to determine if you may even have had a TIA, a minimal stroke, but most likely your symptoms were a reaction to a drop in blood sugar. Your potassium, which is borderline, can cause distracting symptoms, too. Your tests actually duplicate those of a hard-working person with gross body stress and dehydration. But you're from a nursing home, aren't you, so it's probably not that. Ha. Well ... oh, that's right—you don't talk, do you? I'm prescribing an aspirin a day. You will need to monitor your glucose and potassium levels with finger sticks three times a week for one week. Er ... we'll have the nursing home do that for you. You can go home as soon as arrangements can be made."

With that, the doctor was gone.

Home! What a nice ring that sound has ... I wish I had a home to go to, he lamented. *I wonder what Thomas has done with my home ... ?*

A TIA, he reflected. The doctor did not need to explain this, even if he thought Harry might understand. He knew that a transient ischemic accident occurs when the brain does not get enough oxygen. A small blood clot enters the brain and only temporarily slows blood flow. After the clot passes through the brain, the person usually returns to normalcy. If a blood clot is too large to go through the vessels and the blood flow stops, a full-blown stroke occurs. Now he recalled that just before he became very weak, he had fuzzy vision and the light hurt his eyes. Probably the sweating, the increased heart rate, and the heavy breathing came as a result of nerves, he reasoned. He had forgotten that abnormal potassium and/or blood sugar levels could in some cases mimic TIA symptoms.

Chapter Twelve ~ 77

Upon his arrival back to "The Haven," for old and handicapped sojourners, the nursing personnel all welcomed him like a long lost friend. The nursing supervisor entered his room, pulled up a chair, and sat down beside him.

"I have the information the hospital sent. Preliminary reports, including your history and physical findings, suggest you may have had a mini stroke. The symptoms you presented could also be indicative of other diagnoses. The possibilities for hypoglycemia, low blood sugar level, and/or hypokalemia, or low potassium level, were evaluated. The doctor thinks your test results point to one of these three possibilities because the report of your initial Magnetic Resonance Arteriogram was negative. So he prescribed an aspirin a day, glucose monitoring every other day for ten days, and potassium test in one week. You are also to eat at least one banana daily for your potassium. You were borderline dehydrated when you were admitted to Memorial. I know these are technical words, Harry, but the bottom line is that in the doctor's opinion and in light of all your test results, you did not have a TIA. Is that good news or what? I have seen this in heavy sweating, hard-working men. That couldn't be you, could it, Harry?" she chuckled. *If she only knew*, he thought to himself, smiling.

"We need to get more fluids in you, also."

The good news made him a little lightheaded with happiness. He did not want another stroke or a heart attack. He had been working out night after night and was losing a lot of body fluid. He tried to drink a lot of water and juice.

That is probably what happened, he reasoned, *and I am responsible for it. I wish I had a water container I could take with me. Next time I go to the darkened hallway, I will search for a drinking fountain.*

He lay on his bed for a long time analyzing his situation. He was deep in thought when Kathy entered and he did not realize she was intently watching his facial expressions as he pondered this latest incident. When he suddenly became aware of another's presence, he turned his head and found himself staring into the eyes that made his heart flutter.

"Kathy," he said softly, then looked around to make sure he was not being overheard. He reached out his hand, folded it around hers, and gave it a gentle squeeze. Obvious to both, the handholding lasted longer than a normal shake. She was smiling and carefully asked questions as she released her hand from his.

"So, my friend, how are you? Needless to say, I was very concerned when I heard you went to the emergency room and had to spend the night in the hospital. Paul and Sari have been relentless in their questions regarding you. They started on their bikes to the hospital, but when I told them you were to be released today, they agreed to wait and visit you here after school. If you are up to it, they will be here this afternoon. I'm afraid that neither elephants nor wild horses could prevent them from visiting you as soon as possible."

It warmed his heart to think of such affection building between him and the children.

"I am fine now," he managed to say.

"Yes, I know. I've been in touch with the nurse, who has kept me posted on your condition. Do you understand what happened to you?"

"Yes, I understand, and before you start scolding, let me say I know that nothing could have prevented a possible TIA and that the conservative treatment is an aspirin a day." A noise caused him to look around the room again. "I also know that a glass of grape juice daily acts as a blood thinner. I have a slight correction to my previous statement, if you please. There are preventive measures that can be taken besides daily grape juice or aspirin. No liquor or tobacco. Nutritious meals without animal fat, regular exercise—conservative, of course," he smiled, then continued, "plenty of fresh water besides a variety of nuts, fruits, vegetables, and legumes. And leading the list of things to do is trust in divine power." He ended with an all-knowing grin that she thankfully returned.

"More probable than having a TIA is that I most likely experienced a drop in either blood sugar or potassium. Besides, my MRA was negative. You know how persistent I've been at working out. I sweat profusely. So I'll drink more water, eat a banana every day, and everything will return to normal. You'll see."

"I believe you and I know you will put into practice what you've learned," she said. "You know, one of your problems is that you know too much!"

After chatting a few more minutes, Kathy rose to go back to work, but not before once again expressing her concerns for his welfare and cautioning his behavior.

She paused and chose her words carefully as she said, "Harry, you really scared me, you know. The children and I were very worried, but we prayed that God would protect you from a setback in your recovery."

"Thank you, Miss Kathy, you did just the right thing. I appreciate your concern. I did not have a mini stroke. Really, it was either a low blood sugar or low potassium. It's in my chart. Take a look." She looked puzzled, squeezed his arm, leaned over to brush a kiss against his forehead, and, resolving to review his chart, took her leave. "I'll look at the reports," she said, and she was gone.

That same afternoon Paul and Sari arrived to visit with Harry. Paul was the first to enter, with Sari close on his heels. Paul sat down where his mother had been sitting earlier and grabbed Harry's hand. Sari ran to the other side of the bed, crawled right up beside him on the bed, and weaseled her little arm under his neck, and lay there hugging him. No one said anything for several minutes, each calming one's own emotions. It seemed as if all three recovered at the same time, for they all started talking at once.

"Are you all right?" asked Sari.

"How do you feel?" quizzed Paul.

At the same time Harry was trying to say he had missed them and how glad he was to see them again. Eventually, all questions were asked and answered, and the hubbub settled down to sounds of two contented children and one very happy man. A half hour passed quickly, and Sari went to see her Mom. This interlude from "motor mouth" gave Harry and Paul time to talk about the "project."

Paul endeavored to give Harry a step-by-step process he had followed on putting the device together and ended by announcing he had everything done except putting on a few more braces, lubricating the wheels, and installing a well-padded cushion.

While Harry was imagining what this thing looked like, Paul was saying, "I think we can bring it in on Sunday, that is, if Mom and I can get the rear seat out of the van."

Paul was anxious to finish this new creation of his and Harry's, so after getting assurance that Harry was going to be all right, he excused himself and biked home while Sari rode with her mother.

Harry realized he had been overextending and overexerting himself by trying to regain strength faster than his body allowed. He was glad to know the "project" Paul was working on was nearly complete, because it would allow him more gentle, consistent exercise to increase his endurance. Since the hospital episode, he had not been out of bed and had made only necessary limited movements within the bed. He knew he had digressed. To some degree, he would have to start his exercise program all over again, however, he felt ready and anxious to continue his program.

Chapter Thirteen

For the most part, the residents had few visitors, and the weekends seemed especially long and lonesome. Harry thought back on the years he had spent in the military. Mail call was a high time; everyone stood around anxiously and eagerly awaiting that precious contact with home and loved ones. His mind vividly recalled the scenes of GIs standing alone without a letter. It was common at that point to see another soldier lead his buddy to one side and share his letter. He smiled as he recalled that in those times, the married men even appreciated letters from their mother-in-law. Returning to the present, he saw the similarity with his fellow residents.

This evening as he sat by the nurses' station observing the customary humdrum, he observed Pete in his usual place doing the same thing he always did, just observing. The nurses were busy. Some were dealing with mounds of paperwork, while others organized medicine carts and passed medicines. Aides were scurrying about carrying loads of sheets and absorbing pads in their arms in an effort to prepare residents for bedtime. The jangling of telephones, residents' calls, moans, and shouts from a nearby room added to the daily routine sounds of nursing home life.

And there was Gertrude waiting for a promised telephone call. The nurse had told her that her daughter would call at eight o'clock tonight. She rarely called. Immediately after supper Gertrude rolled her wheelchair very close to the telephone, got out, and reseated herself as close as she could get, eager anticipation written all over her face.

It was now about fifteen minutes until the appointed time. She was nervous, restless, and fidgety. She could barely sit still and squirmed from side to side in her wheelchair as she wrung her hands. Facial expressions went from eager anticipation to sadness then back to a question mark as she frequently glanced at the telephone.

At eight o'clock the telephone remained silent. She reached for the hand piece knowing the telephone did not ring but thinking that perhaps by her touching it, it would ring. She willed it to ring. It was now 8:05. She locked her chair, stood up, and with building anxiety paced around her chair. She was only one step away from the telephone, but not wanting to be out of reach of the expected call, made a hasty retreat. She now stood staring at the telephone, willing it to ring. Eight-fifteen. No call yet. She sat down but quickly stood, looked for a tissue, and worried it.

Within minutes the tissue was crushed, smoothed, and strangled until it finally became confetti encircling her. Eight-thirty. No call. More shredded tissue. Now nose blowing and watering eyes commenced. She stood … she sat back down. The last time her daughter called was six months ago. The telephone rang, and she lunged for it. Dial tone. It was the nurse's telephone that had rung. Seated now with slumped shoulders, she bowed her snow-white head into her wrinkled hands that lovingly cradled, bathed, dressed, fed, and comforted her daughter, and tears flowed freely. Her shoulders rose and fell. A moan was heard, and then crying in earnest began. An old heart, which freely overflowed with love to her daughter, was being broken.

Harry was witness to a human heart being crushed. Didn't anyone care? Where were the sons, daughters, and loved ones of these seemingly forgotten fathers, mothers, grandparents, and friends. Harry's aching heart cried out in silence for them. He could not contain his emotions. Reaching up to rub a tickle on his face, his hand came away wet. Silent tears for the old lady were dripping off his chin.

He had to leave the scene, but before he did, he noticed Rozlyn, the evening nurse who had alerted diminutive Gertrude, affectionately know as Gertie, of her forthcoming telephone call. She was seated at the nurse's station busy with paperwork. However, she was not too involved to keep an eye on Gertie. Rozlyn too had seen Gertie's anxiety. She observed her nervousness. She witnessed the fidgeting. She had experienced this display of hurt and disappointment repeatedly with many residents. Rozlyn was full of love and compassion. She knew what to do to help prevent a possible catastrophe. With a sad face and moist eyes, the kind, tenderhearted, overworked, underappreciated, and underpaid nurse rose, approached Gertie, and laid a sympathetic hand on her shoulder. Her own face distorted with tears, she attempted a smile as she looked into those old, watery eyes, knelt down in front of the wheelchair, and gave Gertie an extended hug.

They rocked back and forth, neither able to speak. What could be said? Finally, the nurse arose, went to the back of the wheelchair, leaned forward over the heartbroken old mother, and, with arms pressed around Gertie's shoulders, placed her hands on the arms of the chair. And while still embracing her, she moved her wheelchair behind the nurses' station, where she continued with her paperwork for a long time, all the while speaking softly and tenderly to Gertie.

This incident reminded him of another situation that had occurred the previous week. Harry was in his usual place, observing. State inspectors were examining charts, schedules, and treatment plans and were busily talking with the director of nurses. Julia, a resident, always walked the corridors but mostly hung out near the nurses' station. She clucked and moaned. Spittle clung to her chin, as did unnatural hair. Her shapeless dress covered her skinny and shapeless body.

She had a special fondness for Virginia, the nursing director. As the inspectors engaged Virginia in discussion, Julia continually made sounds of whimpering and groaning and the ever-present clucking. She kept returning to stand beside Virginia, who accepted this behavior as though it was natural. In fact, Virginia would occasionally glance toward Julia and give her a smile of acknowledgment.

The inspectors were not amused and sent scowls toward Julia as often as Virginia smiled at her. With what seemed like barely controlled aggravation, they suddenly asked Virginia if she could do something about this annoyance. It was then that Virginia looked up and spoke to Julia.

"Hi Julia," she said. Are you looking for me?" She arose, stepped toward Julia, and said, "This is what you are looking for, isn't it?" And she gave her a hug and a cuddle.

Julia immediately resumed another shuffle around the halls. The inspectors looked chagrined.

"All she wanted was a little love," Virginia explained to embarrassed faces.

On Sunday afternoon, when the nursing home was quietest, Paul and his mom entered the back door of the nursing home struggling with the new "ZYCLE," as Paul named it. It could have passed as just another piece of physical therapy equipment, but Harry was glad no one saw them struggling as it was moved into the physical therapy department. There was a little back room in the department that was used mostly for storage, and that is where the ZYCLE came to a rest.

Harry looked at it with awe while Paul beamed. His eyes moved from Harry to the ZYCLE and then back to Harry. The silence was deafening and extended so long Paul was beginning to think Harry did not like what he saw. Exuberant, effervescent Sari felt compelled to break the silence.

"Well?" she exclaimed. Paul's expectant expression gradually turned worried as he looked at Harry, who licked his dry lips, closed his gaping mouth, and started to grin, a smile that matured to a significant belly laugh.

They looked from one to another and back to this one-of-a-kind hybrid, and they all laughed with excited giddiness. If there had not been two doors between this little group and the corridor, someone passing would have certainly heard the commotion and entered. Harry's emotions were mixed as he gazed at the ZYCLE. He was so very proud of Paul, who, at just shy of thirteen, was thorough in his understanding of what Harry needed and, with his young ability, fabricated a fine piece of exercise equipment. Kathy's face showed motherly pride for her son and happiness for Harry.

Chapter Thirteen — 83

"OK, Paul, explain how this contraption works," Harry lightheartedly quipped.

"Yeah, well. You see, I have basically taken two bicycles and altered them to fit our needs," he explained. Both Harry and Kathy could not help but notice the grown-up attitude Paul exhibited.

One's first impression would be that it resembled a tandem bicycle, but Paul had shortened the front frame considerably. He had fashioned "outriggers" in the front and rear for stability. Handlebars were somewhat intact on the front frame. Instead of a seat, he had integrated his body board covered with a soft mat, so upon mounting, Harry could lie face down with his feet in stirrup pedals. His arms could reach forward and down to where his hands could grasp the pedals on the front sprocket. A chain connected both front and rear sprockets.

Paul explained the reason behind its construction and features. "Your right side is stronger so it can propel the weak side." He had made the whole device low to the floor for easy mounting. "Here, let me demonstrate. I think it would be best for you to approach from behind like this. It's probably hard for you to swing a leg up over the mat, so go to the rear and straddle the back wheel. Then move forward to the mat on which you will lie face down. Before lying forward, sit on the braced back fender and wiggle your left foot into this old cut-down boot. Now lay forward on the mat and with your right hand secure the left hand in this specially designed holder mounted to the pedal. Put your right hand on the front pedal and the right foot on the back pedal like this. Then by pedaling just like a bicycle, the right hand and right leg will propel the weakened side. Now you give it a try," he said while hopping off and looking eagerly for Harry's response.

Harry wheeled himself close to the rear end of this exceptional product of two inventive minds and, with the aid of his cane, stood up. With a little effort, he straddled the device and moved forward, lack of coordination showing. By sitting down on the braced rear fender, he could rest. With his right hand he picked up the left leg and aimed the socked foot into the boot. He had to reach over to coordinate its entry. He then leaned forward and pulled himself onto the mat and lay forward. With his right hand he positioned his left hand on the pedal and secured it with Velcro, which Paul had thoughtfully attached. He lay there for a moment to catch his breath, hoping, praying, and wondering if this would be the miracle device he had hoped for.

Harry expected some wobbling, but the ZYCLE was surprisingly stable. He thought it amazing how Paul had cut, bent, lengthened this and shortened that, added, welded, and finally painted until it was a viable piece of equipment. ZYCLE was Paul's name for this piece of handiwork. It seemed to be properly labeled for its intended use. "Exercise with a modified bicycle," Paul stated.

Harry looked at all four extremities, making sure the left ones were secured and commenced pedaling, slowly at first and then with increased speed. He slowed down, and Paul walked closer, squatted down by the sprocket, and said, "See this knob?" Harry nodded. Paul continued, "You turn it clockwise to increase tension, which will make it harder to pedal and turn it counterclockwise to decrease the tension. You will want to increase it as you get stronger."

"This boy has thought of everything," Harry marveled. Kathy was standing on the sideline surveying the scene. She was savoring the moment when Paul had the chance to make something practical and useful. He had made many contraptions, for which she always encouraged him by expressing her interest and understanding. She was pleased that finally he had made a purposeful, presentable, usable fixture, and seeing Harry's gratitude and appreciation made her happy. She beamed with pleasure as Paul showed Harry each thing he had altered and fabricated, the reason for it and how it worked. Even Sari sat quietly in evident awe, not having a thing to say for the moment.

With renewed sadness, Kathy realized how much Paul needed a father figure in his life. She recognized that the two were getting quite close and realized Paul had come to love Harry dearly. You could tell by his freedom of thought and relaxed expression. Harry acted genuinely interested in Paul as well. Harry, Kathy noted, was very guarded with his feelings. His reluctance toward expressing his emotions was probably a result of being abandoned by his wife and son and their rejection of his love. She could well understand his reticence, because an unloving husband had dumped her, too. But children, she thought, are innocent and anxious to please, to love and accept at face value.

Kathy's professionalism, her awareness for caution and safety, gave vent. "You will have to be very careful with this unproven contraption. It looks good and I have a lot of confidence in Paul but, Harry, you must be very careful, for it is as yet untried … unproven. It could be weakened by usage and you could inadvertently fall and get hurt." Paul shot his mother a disgruntled look, but she continued to address Harry. "You also have a tendency to go overboard with your sometimes uncontrolled haste and enthusiasm. Just because you can mount this by yourself and can exercise at your convenience, doesn't mean you should do it all the time. After all, remember what sent you to hospital last time."

Now it was time for Harry to look sober. Mock sober. He cast a rueful look toward Paul, who was staring at him, and they both, trying to be inconspicuous, frowned but rolled their eyes, turned their heads, smiled, and listened as Kathy continued. "You do have a handicap, you know. You can generally come in here and exercise when I am in the next room seeing patients, but I have the only key to the PT area, so you might say I am in control. I am going to give you a duplicate key and while you are free to use this room, you must use discretion and exercise in moderation. Do you hear me, Harry Tucker?" She used his full name when she saw he and Paul, again, giving one another amused looks.

"Yes, Mother," they chimed in unison, nodding and trying to look very grave. The scene produced its needed effects, and her bemused smile indicated she also felt her words of caution would go unheeded but had to be said nevertheless. She made him practice several more times to mount and dismount by himself. Kathy proudly placed her arm on Paul's shoulder and said they must hurry to the church picnic, which was already in progress. They left Harry beside the ZYCLE.

He fingered the key she had given him, and although the maiden trial of the ZYCLE left him sweating, he thought he would give it another try before returning to his room.

After ten minutes he was tired and quite ready to quit, for it was nearly suppertime anyway. He certainly did not want to draw the nurses' attention and cause them to worry about his wanderings.

The use of the new ZYCLE was paying off. After three weeks of moderate exercise, he could once again control the coordination of both his left arm and left leg. He was ready to increase his workout. When he went to the physical therapy's back room, he took along his Bible and other reading material. Paul's body board was long enough for Harry to prop up a book and read while doing his routine. He resumed his outside sorties as well. He was determined to get away from his present surroundings. His mind was active, and his body was restless. The stronger he became, the more anxious he was to be independent again. Practicing the health rules of nature was producing its promised benefits as well.

Four weeks passed without incident, and for two of those weeks, he had been walking the darkened hallway nightly. Outdoors he would take deep breaths of fresh air. The sunshine was darkening his skin. He was taking on a healthy glow. No one seemed to notice, however, except Kathy and her children.

Alone in his ZYCLE room, he would practice dressing and undressing. He could now take care of himself unassisted. But because he did not want the aides to know of his growing independence, some of the personal care routines ended up being redundant. He did not want his returning capabilities revealed, so he was still being aided with getting dressed, tying his shoes, and brushing his teeth, to name a few. He thought it interesting that none of his attendants really seemed to notice his firming muscles and healthy glow. He felt because he had been labeled a disabled person, the staff was neither looking for nor expecting any improvement.

His anxiety was building and he became obsessed with getting out of the nursing home. He rehearsed multiple scenarios for departure. Where would he go? What would he do? Where would he stay? So many questions persistently occupied his thinking, and slowly answers came to his stroked mind, which was becoming more active and responsive. He was mentally formulating plans. He did not forget he had been stripped of all identification. He had no driver's license, no social security card, no credit cards, no cash, nothing. He would have to be careful where he went, for he had no way of proving he was Harry Tucker.

Thomas had taken all his personnel belongings as well. He had no clothes except leftovers from the laundry room. He had rummaged through the unclaimed clothes during the long nights and found some barely acceptable items. Shoes were a big problem, but he found a right and a left of different styles that nevertheless were close in color and size. He found black shoe polish and tried to make them the same shade. The result was not fashionable, but they were the best he could find. Many ideas flooded his brain as to how to leave with the least amount of attention. Perhaps he should talk this over with Kathy one of these days. No! Soon, maybe. He then thought he should avoid any embarrassing situations. The fewer the people who knew of his plans, the fewer answers they would have if asked about his whereabouts.

The next day as he was using the ZYCLE, Kathy entered the little room and sat down in the only chair. He was so thankful for this lady. She had truly been a godsend. *Didn't God say, "I will never leave you or forsake you." He uses people to accomplish His designs*, thought Harry. *He has sent her into my life—what would I have done without her?*

"What are you thinking about?" she asked. "Looks like either a mischievous or serious expression in your eyes."

He stopped his incessant pedaling, sat up, and with a somber expression stated, "I am ready to leave this place." She was only mildly startled and stood up. She had sensed this coming but was not ready for it.

"What do you mean?" She knew the answer but needed the interlude to think.

"I am as ready as I'll ever be. Only you know of my true condition. I can walk, talk, dress, shave, comb my hair, and take care of all my personal needs and more. I have been practicing writing also. Last night as I was passing the maintenance room, I noticed the door unlocked, so I entered and altered my cane."

It was only then that Kathy noticed that his cane leaning against his wheelchair was not standing by itself. The four legs were missing. He had ground them all off. One night, he explained, as he was going to the darkened hallway, he had passed the maintenance room. The door was ajar, but the light was off. He peeked in and then wheeled himself in, then closed and locked the door. Surveying the area, his eyes came to rest on the grinder. An idea popped into his head. When he finished with the grinder, he was left with a single-legged chrome cane.

"I see," was all she could say.

He continued, "I have thought of many different ways to leave without raising a lot of questions, but as independent as I want to be, I need help. However, you must not do anything that would compromise your status."

She sat with her mouth slightly agape as he disclosed several options and settled on what he considered a workable one. She had some suggestions, but she agreed she could not get involved. She could neither surrender professional ethics nor employment regulations. This was a dilemma for her.

In a little more than a year's time, Harry had progressed from an unconscious, non-communicative, non-thinking, bedfast mass of bones and protoplasm requiring total care, to a thinking, talking, erect form bursting with moderate strength but with tenacious independence. He seemed to read her thoughts and assured her that however his plans materialized, they would in no way reflect on her. She hesitatingly agreed but said she would talk with him more about it.

Chapter Fourteen

On the forthcoming holiday, the administrative offices would be closed. The work atmosphere would be relaxed. Employees would take longer breaks, and the nurses would be less attentive.

Kathy had free access to patient charts and patient records. His chart would be quite bulky, but she found the discharge forms, placed them in his chart, and folded over the corners for easy identification. When the nurses went on their break, he wheeled himself behind the nurses' desk and reached for a thick chart. It was his.

"What do you think you are doing?" called an aide. He nearly dropped his teeth as his heart leaped into his throat. The aide rushed on past to help Pete as he tried to stand and was swaying, ready to fall.

"Phew!" that was close, he mumbled. He quickly found the papers, shoved them inside his shirt, and proceeded to his secret ZYCLE room.

Once inside, he locked the door, took a deep breath of relief, and wiped sweat from his brow. He reasoned that what he was doing was not wrong, only appropriating procedures to his own advantage. After his nerves quieted, he extracted a pen and worked on filling out his discharge forms. When all was completed, he replaced them inside his gown pocket and mounted his ZYCLE, perhaps for the last time. While pedaling, he dreamed of life outside the nursing home.

He waited anxiously for the afternoon break when he could place the discharge forms in his chart—his ticket to freedom. There was the usual hubbub of staff coming and going at shift change. When all the daytime staff had gone and he thought the parking lot was vacant of day-shift cars, he crawled out of bed, slid into his wheelchair, and tried not to look like he was in a hurry. Suppressing his obvious attitude of joy, he made his way to the physical therapy room.

In eager anticipation of his pending escape, he had frequented the laundry room several more times and located two changes of clothing from the discard bin and had stored them in the exercise room. He now dressed and placed all the appropriated items in the knapsack Paul had provided for his use and walked down the vacated office corridor and out the front door as though he had a perfect right to do so. And he did. He could have been mistaken for a visitor, unless one closely inspected his mismatched clothes and shoes.

Through the entrance, down the sidewalk, and out onto the street he strolled. He slowed down a bit to conserve energy and found himself attempting to whistle a tune through crooked lips, something he had not been able to do since before his stroke. He had not felt so good about himself for a long time. He was so happy, he ducked his head, smiled, or spoke greetings to everyone he met along the sidewalk. He knew he looked quite like a derelict or a refugee, but the few pedestrians he passed seemed too busy to notice.

He turned a corner to get off the main street leading to the nursing home. "No need to raise unnecessary suspicions," he said to himself. The sun was bright, the air was fresh, the birds were singing, and he was praising the Lord. He walked and walked. As fatigue gradually overtook him, he looked for a place to rest. Harry spotted a park just up ahead and slumped onto a bench, knowing his tiredness was due to nerves as well as the unaccustomed distance he walked.

Evening was approaching. He had not thought of eating until just now when his stomach growled a demanding reminder. He pulled out some crackers along with a small can of juice, which he had saved from his lunch tray, and ate hungrily. The snack gave him a boost of energy, but he soon realized it was not going to hold him for long.

He watched with loving interest as two young boys cavorted around their mother, teasing one another as they walked along the sidewalk. They reminded him of his own children, which made him wonder how or if they would fit into his future or how he would fit into theirs. Heather should be returning home in a few months, if his memory of her school status was accurate. Where would she live? When Thomas sold his dad's house, he sold the home Heather used to live in before she went to school. True, college and advanced studies had taken her away for a couple of years, but home base was her dad's house.

His rest, his observation of nature, his people watching and his contemplations had taken up more time than he expected. Night was coming on, and he did not have so much as a newspaper to cover him should he happen to go to sleep on a park bench or under a shrub. He got up and started walking with no particular destination in mind.

After several blocks he found he was back within sight of the nursing home. He approached the back entrance and was startled when he heard, "Hey, whatcha doing out here? Ya' got new threads, I see." It was Big Jim out for an evening smoke. "Got your voice back too."

"Hi, where's Mona?" Inquiring about her would distract Big Jim's questioning.

"Finishing her supper. Had yours?"

"No, not yet. What was served?"

"Meatloaf, smashed potatoes, and salad."

Harry felt some of the gnawing in his stomach leave.

"Hear about Old Sam?" asked Big Jim.

"No, what about him?"

"He cashed out this afternoon. The meat wagon just took him away. It was not a sad affair. He was 104 years old and had outlived his entire family and friends. He had no one to grieve over him. Must have been a lonesome man."

"Aren't we all," Harry said.

"Yeah, guess so."

Old Sam lived in the corner room by the rear entrance and Harry could see the nursing assistants through the window cleaning his room and changing bed linens. An idea entered his mind that he might have a warm room for the night after all.

"Goin' in now, Harry?"

"I'll enjoy the evening air for a little while and then I'll go in," he answered. Big Jim went in to be with Mona, and Harry went to the patio, where he sat and contemplated his next move. While he was extremely happy to be discharged, his future was still uncertain. He needed money, food, and lodging as soon as possible.

Late evening came, and darkness soon enveloped the nursing home grounds and building. He guessed patients had been put to bed, after which the staff took their breaks. He entered the back door just before it was scheduled to be locked, and, noticing no one in the corridor, dashed around the corner and into Old Sam's room. His was the bed by the window, so Harry closed the window blind and pulled the privacy curtain between the beds so that if someone were to look in from the hallway, he could not be seen. He happily saw that the former occupant's food tray had not been touched. He ate what he could from it.

He slept well and was quite pleased with the events of day one.

At breakfast time the day shift as usual brought trays to the rooms of patients who needed eating assistance. He lay on his side facing away from the door and pulled the covers nearly over his head. As was the rule, trays were passed, and when time permitted, bed patients were fed. Sam's room was at the end of the corridor and very close to the kitchen, which meant that he would be one of the first to be served a tray of food and among the last to receive help. By the time the aide came in to assist Old Sam, Harry had eaten and was leaving through the back door, where he overheard two aides talking on their way to the dining room.

"Too bad about Old Sam. I will miss him."

"Wh-what do you mean? What happened? I took a tray to him this morning, and he looked all right. Sleeping."

"You got to be kidding. He died yesterday afternoon!"

"Wait! Just a minute." She stopped, turned around, and hustled to his room and cautiously peered in.

"Come here—and quick," she directed her co-worker.

The bed was nicely made and the food tray was pilfered. The aide momentarily turned pale and backed out of the room, muttering something unintelligible. Harry could not risk listening to more of their conversation and hastened outside, smiling as he went.

His day was commencing with a bit of levity that made him feel like part of the outside world. As he cautiously exited the front gate, he turned to see what he hoped would be his last glimpse of Haven Hills Nursing and Rehabilitation Center. Perhaps he would return as a visitor sometime but certainly not as a patient, not if he could help it. It was not because he did not receive good care. The nurses and staff were commendable. For the most part, they were loving, kind, and committed to patient comfort and contentment. But at this point in his life, he was too independent to enjoy someone fussing over him.

Standing beside the gate looking at the facility from the front, he noted its attractive aesthetic features: its circular drive surrounding a fountain with a waterfall and the attractive, eye-catching brick walls encasing hand-carved double wooden front doors. Larry did an exquisite job with the gardening and with maintaining a beautiful landscape.

Facing the street and the real world held him captive but for a moment. The feeling of freedom could be enjoyed later. He sped away as fast as his two legs would carry him. Although one was weak and he had not yet overcome a moderate limp, he made good time in getting several blocks between him and the nursing home.

After crossing several intersections, he slowed his pace, leaned against a stone wall to rest and to observe the neighborhood activities. There were children in one yard with a young woman, presumably their mother, who was intermittently reading while overseeing her children's play. A couple of houses down were two elderly gents passing the time of day by watching traffic and pedestrians hurrying by. One became rather animated describing some situation. It must have been an exciting story, judging from the rise in his voice.

A dog barked in the yard behind him, bringing him back to the present, and he proceeded on down the street.

He soon came upon an elderly woman standing in her driveway and trying to start her lawnmower. She would pull the starter rope, and the engine would sound as if it wanted to start but would sputter and fail. By the time he drew alongside the entrance, he could see the look of defeat and discouragement on the old woman's face, so he ventured into the drive. She saw him drawing near, straightened up the best she could, and drew back slightly. He looked safe enough, she thought to herself, except for those horrible clothes.

Perhaps he was with the circus. Maybe he was a street person. When he smiled, she felt a little more at ease and tried to look benevolent.

"Looks like it does not want to go to work today," he said. "Some days I feel like that myself."

The lady could certainly relate to that statement and said, "I have tried and tried to start this thing for two days, and it absolutely refuses to run."

"I'd be happy to give it a go if you would like me to."

"Would you, please, if it is not too much bother?"

"I'll just look at some of the possible simple problems and go from there."

"Fine. You do that and I'll get some lemonade. It is so hot today."

He gave the machine a cursory inspection, then checked the gas level. Just as he suspected, no gas. He found a can in the garage beside an old but beautifully kept Lincoln Continental. He filled the tank, opened the choke, and on his second try, the engine coughed a few times and then purred nicely. He switched the engine off as the woman waddled out of the house with two glasses of juice, one of which she handed to him.

"My name is Harry Tucker."

"And mine is Sadie Grimbolt. It's nice to know you, Mr. Tucker, and however will I pay you for your trouble?"

"You already have, Mrs. Grimbolt," he said as he lifted his glass of juice and smiled.

"My arthritis has worsened over the years, and in the last few weeks, it has practically stopped me from working. I have tried and tried to get help to keep my lawn mowed and shrubs pruned. Several men have come, but no one stays long. I just cannot find responsible helpers. Maybe I am too critical, but I do insist on honesty and a fair day's work for a fair day's wage."

"Responsibility is more rare than it used to be," he agreed.

"Let me try this mower here on your front yard just to make sure it will run OK."

He pulled the starter and followed the mower around the yard. It was a good-sized yard, he soon realized. As he trailed the push mower, he reflected on the neighborhood he had limped into. It was obviously inhabited by affluent residents. The houses were large and seemingly well cared for.

After completing several trips around the yard, he was convinced that apart from an empty gas tank, the mower had no other problems and worked just fine. He knew now that he could not leave the lawn partially mowed.

"The mower is working just fine, Mrs. Grimbolt, would you like to test it?

"I would love to, but as I said earlier, my arthritis prevents me just now."

"If you wish, I will complete the job."

"I would be forever grateful if you would. Am I imposing on you? Surely you have more to do than help an old woman."

"I assure you, this is all I have to do this afternoon."

She crept back into the house, and Harry spent the better part of a half hour to complete the job. When he finished, he filled the gas tank and pushed it around the side of the garage and into the backyard. What met his eyes really surprised him. The yard was massive. *She does all this with a push mower*, he exclaimed in his thoughts. *She needs a riding mower, unless she uses the push mower for the exercise.*

He saw a variety of a dozen or more fruit trees, some laden with fruit, as well as hedges, shrubs, a flower garden, a few vegetables growing, an out barn and a greenhouse. *Some energy this woman has!* he concluded. While he was still in thought, Mrs. Grimbolt came out the back door with another glass of lemonade and limped up behind him.

"Do you like my place?"

"Yes, but how on earth do you keep it looking so nice with your arthritis hurting and all?"

"That's why I have tried to get help. I mow a little every day of the week."

"Would you be willing that I go around this a few times? Maybe it would be helpful to you."

"Are you sure you want to tackle such a job? The front yard looks better than it has for a long time," she sighed.

He took her answer for a yes, saying, "I'll see what I can do."

He finished the cool drink, started the mower, and took off. Each time he rounded the yard and neared the house, he saw Mrs. Grimbolt peeking around the curtains. One time he thought he saw her smiling. *If she's happy, I'm happy.*

He had worked up quite a sweat long before he finished, and exhaustion was quickly overtaking him. He now realized he should not have been so generous with his initial enthusiasm. He talked to the Lord about needing a little extra strength to finish the job, and He answered.

Mrs. Grimbolt had gotten into her car and left. When he finished and saw that she had not yet returned, he found pruning shears and branch clippers in the greenhouse and went to work manicuring the flowers and shrubbery. When she returned, he saw her enter the house with bags in tow. Shortly, she appeared at his side.

"I'm preparing a little bite to eat. Will you join me?"

He was by now feeling quite drained of strength, and his muscles were trembling from having expended more energy than he had in store. *The Lord is taking care of me yet again*, he acknowledged. His stomach had been talking around the fast disappearing lemonade.

"Why, yes, ma'am, if it isn't too much trouble."

"It's no trouble at all, and don't worry, eating is not the only pay you will get for doing such a marvelous job."

Before he could answer, she turned and ambled into the house, calling over her shoulder, "Come in when you are finished."

Over mashed potatoes, peas, a filet of salmon, sweet corn, and more lemonade, they talked.

"You happened along at just the right time, Mr. Tucker."

"You can say that again!" he exclaimed, leaning back and patting his stomach.

"What do you mean?"

"Well, ah, oh, ah, you see, I am by myself and don't cook."

Mrs. Grimbolt had been around long enough to know there was a story behind that hesitation, but she did not pry. Those clothes did not fit his speech. He would explain if and when he wanted to.

"My husband died last year, but I love this old place. I know it is more than I should try to maintain. I could sell and go to an old folks' home."

Her aged, lined face took on a sad expression. He felt her emotions and said, "Don't rush it," his own recent experiences showing on his face.

He quickly recovered and heard her say, "If I could find good help, I think I could manage for a while longer."

"I'm sure you could. But one thing is certain; you would do well by getting a riding mower. What now takes three or four hours, you yourself could do it in less than an hour."

"I know, but I don't know anything about riding mowers—and very little about push mowers, as you found out today."

The subject was dropped as the doorbell sounded. Her neighbor from a block away stopped by to check on her aged friend and was surprised and amused to see a strange man sitting at her table.

"Well, who do we have here?"

We. I wonder if she is a nurse, he reflected ... thinking back to former comments by the nurse in the home.

"Lillian, meet Mr. Tucker. He's been a tremendous help to me today. My lawn mower would not start, and with my arthritis acting up, I did not know what I was going to do. He fixed the mower, mowed both the front and backyard, pruned, trimmed my trees and shrubs. My place looks better than it has for months."

"I wish I had someone to take care of mine," Lillian said as she extended her hand to Harry.

"Nice to meet you Mrs.... ." Harry responded offering his hand.

"Oh, just call me Lillian, everybody does," she hastily interjected.

"Thank you. Perhaps with a satisfactory recommendation from Mrs. Grimbolt, I could help you."

"Yes, yes, of course, Mr. Tucker. I just don't want Lillian stealing you away from my needs. And, goodness, call me Sadie. I'm not an old woman yet."

When Sadie hobbled away with hands full of dishes, he could feel Lillian's piercing eyes, analyzing him. She had not seen his limp, but she could tell from his clothes that he was not dressed like a gardener. Rather, he looked more like a vagabond, and his speech was better than a common laborer's. *Probably a vagrant. Sadie had better keep an eye on this one. I sure will.*

The fact is, I'm dressed worse than a common laborer in this neighborhood, he pondered.

"Tomorrow, then, Mr. Tucker? Here's my address."

He gingerly took the gold embossed business card she handed him, hoping not to smear it.

"Thank you Mrs … ah, Lillian. It's been nice to meet you. I had better go now."

At the door Sadie pressed an envelope into his hand. He tried to protest, knowing it was pay for doing her yard work. His primary interest had been to do a neighborly deed for her, and he did so without thought of remuneration, but Sadie would have nothing to do with his refusal.

"Goodbye, thank you, and I'll see you next week?" She asked, nearly pleading.

"Anytime of the day, OK?"

"At your convenience."

"Goodbye."

"Goodbye." Harry could hear Lillian shouting goodbye from the dining room.

He made his way down the walk into the driveway and momentarily stopped and stared at the uniformed chauffeur leaning against a big black limousine about a block long. He nodded at the non-responsive driver who returned his stare peering down a long arrogant nose at the departing laborer.

Harry was tired. What a day, he thought to himself. He remembered noticing a park a short distance ahead and he made for it. Flopping down on the grass, his fatigued body quickly relaxed and he fell fast asleep. The last thing he remembered, he was praising the Lord for His goodness.

Chapter Fifteen

When Harry rolled over, he felt paper crumpling in his pocket and then remembered the envelope Mrs Grimbolt had insisted on giving him. He gradually awoke from a deep, restful sleep, though his muscles and joints ached from the day's labor and from lying on the damp ground. He opened the envelope and several bills fell out. "Wow! Sixty dollars," he nearly shouted. Passersby gave him a curious stare. He quickly shoved it back into his pocket before anyone could see it. But somebody had. He heard a rustling in the shrubs behind him and felt the cold edge of a knife blade on his throat as an arm surrounded his chest pinning his arms to his sides.

"Give me that money, fat cat."

He could smell the combination of tobacco and cheap liquor on the woman's breath. Hard-earned money. Food. Clothing. Shelter. Thoughts went through his mind like a machine gun. His assailant had been behind the hedge fence probably thinking Harry was a sleeping drunk. Without further thought he broke her hold, swung around, and at the same time grabbed her wrist that held the weapon. His throat let loose a piercing, blood-curdling scream. He was not exactly sure where the yell had come from, but on subsequent walks near the same area, he thought he could still hear it resonating.

The noise and Harry's quick action alarmed his assailant. She quickly turned, dropped the weapon, and fled.

What a day! he thought. *Sixty dollars in his pocket, mugged, and a free knife!* He was still shaking when he decided he should be more careful where he slept next time. He had rested a couple of hours but was still very weary. He was mentally and physically exhausted, and he wondered where he should go. He had not had such a variety of social contacts for more than a year. It was not safe in the park, and he had certainly better not chance the nursing home again. He smiled as he recalled his first night's episode.

Chapter Fifteen ~ 97

Harry stopped by a mom and pop grocery store and purchased two bananas, two apples, a pound of grapes, a box of cold cereal and a bottle of juice. *Better travel light. This should be enough for both supper tonight and breakfast in the morning*, he calculated. With smaller denominations now, he carefully placed six dollars in a safe place. Tithe. His cane had been pressed into service to carry his bag of personal items over his shoulder. He now loosened the rubber handle and removed it. He thought of Gertie who's cane always contained a nip or two. After inserting several bills for safekeeping, he replaced the handle.

Night was approaching. He could feel dew in the air. Where would he sleep tonight?

Approaching a pay phone, he chose to make a stop and give Kathy a call. No one was home, but the answering machine picked up. "You have reached the Carson home. I'm sorry no one is home at the present time, but if you will leave your name and telephone number where you can be reached, we will return your call as soon as we can." That was Paul's recorded voice.

"Hello, Paul, this is Harry. Just wanted to let you know my first day out was a success. Will call again. Bye."

The telephone was ringing when the Carson family walked through the door. Just as Sari put down her schoolbooks and ran to the telephone, she heard "… a success. Will call again. Bye."

She quickly grabbed the handset and shouted, "Harry!" hoping the rise in her voice would make him hear her. But the line went dead, and so did her spirit.

"Mom, that was Harry. Where is he? What will he do? He's out there somewhere all by himself without money, without a place to sleep, and probably without anything to eat!"

She fell into her mother's outstretched arms and wept. Paul could not stop a tear from surfacing and sliding down his cheek as well. Kathy felt helpless.

After moments of anxiety and apprehension over Harry's well-being, they stood holding on to one another. Kathy, endeavoring to ease their concern, said, "Harry is very independent … sometimes stubborn too, but a capable and resourceful person. While these traits of character have helped him rehabilitate, they can be rather provoking, can't they? I offered money, but he refused. I offered him a place here, but he refused, saying it would not look good to the neighbors."

"But what is he going to do, Mommy?" Sari began another wail.

"Mother, let's pray for him right now," Paul said. And all huddled together and prayed a most fervent request for the Father of all to take care of His child and their friend, Harry.

Eyes opened and Kathy said, "This is something he has to do by himself. He needs to prove he is able to care for his own needs."

Out on the main street, Harry stretched out his arm and stuck his thumb up. Either the drivers did not see him or they chose not to acknowledge him. It had been a long time since he had thumbed a ride, and now he wondered if people still did it anymore. He stepped out into the street a little farther so as to be seen and a car came too close as it turned the corner. *Better watch myself.*

A car slowed, the driver gave him a quick glance and sped on. After several more cars passed without looking, a car suddenly stopped.

"Where ya goin', Pop?" The voice came from a teenage boy with a carefree attitude and peach fuzz on his upper lip.

"Going to the airport. You goin' anywheres near it?" He tried to sound cool and careless like his clothes, which appeared to be a far cry from any evidence of sophistication. He was beginning to smell from the day's hard labor at Mrs. Grimbolt's.

"No, but I'll take you there. Just got my driver's license last week and Dad said I could have the car for thirty minutes to practice driving."

Oh, great, thought Harry, *I'm a guinea pig.*

"Which airlines you takin'?" he asked as he sped down the highway.

"Drop me off at the first entrance," he said, not knowing one terminal from the other.

After what seemed like only a minute, the kid announced, "OK, here we are."

"Thanks. What's your name?"

"Chad."

"Tell your dad you drove real good, Chad."

"Thanks. He'll be happy to hear that. Bye."

Harry went through security and was stopped by the buzzer. He passed his cane around the side and re-entered. No problem.

I will be safer in here. No knives. Hey, my knife! I wonder why it was not seen on the X-ray. Safer in here, huh?

He came to a quiet area, found a newspaper, sat down, and pretended to read. The rest felt good. He noticed a canceled airline ticket sticking out of an envelope lying on the floor by his chair. He picked it up, inserted it into his shirt pocket, and looked for all the world like a traveler. He wanted to look the part, not like a vagrant should security happen to walk by. By the time he finished the newspaper, it was rather late and he was exhausted. Finding an area behind a row of seats next to a wall, he eased down onto the floor. It was harder than the ground in the park! He was more tired than the floor was hard, and he dropped off to sleep after saying thank you to the One watching over him.

He ate more of the cold cereal and the remaining fruit for breakfast. He then went to the men's room, where he washed up as best he could, groomed, and then headed for Lillian's place. The ride he found going in the direction of her address dropped him off about two miles short of his destination. The driver must have thought a person dressed like him would not be a typical resident of that community. He did not mind the walk, however, knowing it was good exercise for his leg, and the fresh air was invigorating.

He was impressed with this well-to-do neighborhood. He figured he was close to the area where Mrs. Grimbolt lived, but his approach brought him from a different direction. He marveled at the well-kept yards and incredible looking mansions. He wondered what Lillian's place would be like. He did not have long to think about it as he neared the next intersection, for he recognized the street name to be hers.

Houses on both sides of the street were fabulous. All had security gates, opened only by remote or by guards with special codes. Many yards had swimming pools with expensive looking cars parked in long, circular driveways.

The McKenzie house number was lighted in an arched stone facade, and on either side were iron gates for automobiles to enter and exit. Under the lighted house number, an iron gate allowed walk-through for foot traffic. He pressed the call signal. A suspicious, deep baritone nasal voice intoned, "Yes?" Harry could envision a tall, stoic, self-important, black-clad butler looking down a long, pompous nose screening calls to protect his employer.

"My name is Harry Tucker."

"What is it you desire, sir?"

"Lillian asked me to come today."

"What is the nature of your business, may I ask?"

"I have an appointment at her request."

"Madam McKenzie is resting. Please call later."

"She asked me to come today, and I think we ought not to disappoint her."

A buzzer sounded, and Harry guessed that was the signal to enter the estate. The metal gate automatically opened, then swung shut behind him with a determined bang. Once inside, the expanse opened to a broader view. Under full, leafy branches of the giant, spreading oak trees, he could see a worker handpicking leaves off the ground. On the other side, there were two people kneeling, digging out weeds in flower gardens. As he proceeded to the back, the impeccably groomed campus awed him. He wondered why she asked him to care for her yard. In the background to the east, he saw grape arbors, an orchard of apple trees joined by peach, pear, and other fruit-bearing trees he could not identify from this distance. He heard horses neighing from the back and saw a couple of riders as he cornered the mansion.

On a door under a sign with fading black letters that read, "Employee Entrance," he knocked and was met by Lillian herself.

Still dressed in a satin night robe, she smiled, extended her hand, and said, "Thank you for being prompt, Mr. Tucker." He felt thankful she remembered him. He did not have a gold-embossed card to present.

"What was your first impression of McKenzie Manor? I know you must think I'm a very wealthy woman living in such splendor. Well, I am."

His first impression that she was a talker was shortly confirmed. He was recalling a statement his business economics professor had stated many years before: "Wealth, like everything, is relative. Some of the loneliest people are those with wealth."

"Would J. Paul Getty put you to shame?" he joked.

"Oh, my, no! John and Tooty were guests here just last week."

Harry felt chagrined.

"John gave a detailed description of their penthouse and I certainly do not envy …"

"Sit down, won't you, please, Mr. Tucker."

"Thank you. I'm embarrassed you'd title me 'Mr.' when you prefer the more familiar title of Lillian for yourself."

This man is no gardener, she told herself. *His speech and manners betray it.*

Lillian, Madam McKenzie, as he felt compelled to call her, brought two cups of steaming coffee and sat down across from him at a small table designed for such an occasion.

Through the many windowed sun porch, they overlooked acres and acres of field and pasture with horses of various sizes and colors. There were barns and corrals and exercise pads.

"I had no idea your place was so large—exquisite, actually." What had he gotten himself into?

"Yes, well our ranch is actually several miles to the north. That's where we keep the stock." He was not sure what that meant, but he did not have time to ask because she got right down to business.

"You probably noticed I have people on the grounds working."

"Yes, I saw several folks doing various jobs."

"They badly need supervision. Mr. Reynolds, the gardener whom my husband employed many years ago, fell and broke his hip two months ago, and I doubt he will ever return to responsible employment. He couldn't do much before the accident, but he had been with us so long that we could not put him out. Sadie called me while you were finishing up at her place and said what a marvelous job you had done. So I rushed right over to see for myself. You're not drinking your coffee."

"Thank you very much for your hospitality, but I don't drink coffee. Please don't be offended."

"Brenda, bring two glasses of orange juice, dear," she called to a passing servant.

"I don't drink coffee either. It's bad for anyone. When it is offered to me, I tell them I don't need drugs," she stated. Only then did Harry realize she had not touched her hot drink either.

"My dear husband, Brian McKenzie, died four years ago this month, and he loved this place. He wanted me to keep this big old estate for as long I could take care of it and one day give it to the State Historical Society. I feel the time is fast approaching when I must do that. I'm getting too old to be concerned about all the different aspects of business. I have a lawyer, a CPA, a financial consultant, and a host of others managing my affairs, but still *I* have to counsel with them and I hate the headache of it."

He was not sure why she was telling him all this, but he knew wealthy people were amongst the most lonely and often did not have what you would call friends in whom they could comfortably confide. He could sense she was not content. From the shadow in her eyes and the constant crease in her forehead, he felt it had been a long time since she was really happy.

"Though I know nothing about you except what Sadie said, I discern you are very capable of managing this assignment. Your job description is simple. Supervise the maintenance of McKenzie Manor. You will have about a dozen men and women to keep busy. You will hire and fire. I do not want to worry about that responsibility."

Harry let out an audible sigh. Thinking he was wavering, she continued, "You get a completely furnished cottage and $2,000 a month to begin. There are no expenses attached. You may eat your meals with the rest of us. You also have free use of any of the vehicles … just make sure, first, it isn't already spoken for. Your personal vehicle will be the old Ford truck parked in front of your cottage."

He was at a loss for words, a myriad of thoughts tumbling through his brain. Thinking of Paul and Sari, his first question was, "Can I have visitors?"

"Of course you can. This isn't a jail or a hospital." Harry winced at her uncanny remark, wondering if she knew his background.

"Do you need help moving in?"

He saw her looking intently at him. He choked on a gulp of orange juice.

"Ah, no," he stammered, and then carefully formed his next comment. "There might be something about me you ought to know." He was overwhelmed and thought he was in over his head.

"Sadie is the best judge of character I know," she cut him off. "Tell me any more and I might not want you."

He wondered what the slight smile behind her stern demeanor meant, but he did not venture further.

"I was so much hoping and trusting that you would take the employment that I took the liberty of having a draft made out for part of your first month's salary."

Dumbfounded, he took the proffered envelope and fairly staggered out the door. If he had looked over his shoulder, he would have seen a rare smile on a rich old lady's lips.

"Thank You, Father of humankind. May my hand always stay in Yours."

He followed her instructions the best he could. Things were occurring so quickly, it was hard to concentrate. His mental acuteness was still less than par.

He located his "cottage." It was actually a completely furnished three-bedroom house, one of which had been commissioned for an office. The house was spotless. It had a very efficient, well-appointed modern kitchen, including a garbage compactor. Plush easy chairs and a posh sofa sat on thick-piled carpet. A music center housing a television, surround sound, and other electronic gear he could not identify stood ready. A fireplace occupied a corner of the family room, a stack of wood waiting. The bedrooms were very well furnished with lamps, armoire, desk, and bureau. There was not a particle of dust anywhere. Why did Lillian say she would have a lady clean twice a week? A well-supplied walk-in pantry joined the kitchen.

Outside in "his drive," he noticed the "old Ford truck" madam had referred to was actually a late model four-wheel-drive Toyota pickup. He unpacked his belongings—or, more accurately, he opened a grocery sack. It took him the longest to decide which of the ten drawers he should designate for his half-dozen clothing articles donated by the nursing home laundry. After familiarizing himself with the house, he went outside, got into "his" truck, and took a tour of the grounds. He returned shortly, chagrined at remembering he had no driver's license, so he could not drive outside the estate.

In his office he found appropriate stationery and completed an application for a duplicate operator's license. Having looked up the address of the department of motor vehicles in the telephone book, he soon had a letter ready to mail. While he was about it, he wrote to social security for a verification of his social security number.

Chapter Sixteen

The next morning at eight o'clock, he assembled the maintenance crew. He recognized several he had encountered the previous day. It looked like an international work force. He introduced himself and asked each to give his or her name and what responsibilities he or she had been assigned. He told them briefly what he expected from them and stated what they could expect from him. There had been some confusion with respect to who was responsible for what. Harry saw the need for a coordinating supervisor indeed. He clarified their assignments, and before dismissing them, he complimented them on how well-kept the place looked and encouraged them to continue. He asked that they offer suggestions as to how they could better maintain or improve the appearance of the estate. They seemed pleased and shuffled out.

He walked to a store that offered money orders, bought one to include with his driver's license application, posted his mail, and walked back home.

Back inside the estate, Harry came upon a young man, probably in his twenties, whom he had seen at the workers' meeting; Harry asked his name.

"Mikhail," answered the young man.

Harry responded, "*Dobraye utro*." (Good morning.)

Startled, the young man nodded, smiled, and returned, "*Dobriy dyen*." It was now the time of day to say, Good day. Harry nodded at the polite correction.

"You speak Rrrussian, Mrr. Harrry!"

"You just heard about all I know. Where are you from?"

"Zaoksky, Rrrussia."

"I visited Vladimir once. Nice place. Many differences compared to America, *da*?"

"*Da!*" he said, beginning to feel comfortable in the presence of his new boss. "Some similarities too."

Harry wanted to dialogue more but needed to go.

"Your work looks good. See you later, Misha." Mikhail beamed with pleasure at the familiar nickname, Misha (equivalent to Mickey). When Harry got to know him better, he mused, maybe he would tease and call him Misha Mooshka, reminiscent of "Meeska Mooska, Mickey Mouse."

At the side of the mansion, he came upon two people working with flowers. "*Como estar*," he said.

Both Cubans rose and through darting eyes said, "*Buenos dìas, El Capitàn.*"

"*Mucho trabajo,*" Harry responded.

"*Si, Señor Tucker, mucho* work, but we like eet."

"Fine-looking roses you've produced."

Harry made the rounds to each laborer, inspecting his or her work and offering encouragement.

The day passed quickly and evening came. After a nice long, warm shower, he fell into bed totally spent, not even bothering to eat supper (*dinner*, using mansion language).

Several days later, awakening early, he lay quietly, thinking of Kathy and her children. He hopped out of bed and telephoned in hopes that she had not left for work yet. "Hello, Carsons." It was Kathy.

"Hello, it's Harry."

"Harry, where are you?"

In the background he could hear that the mention of his name caused a stir.

"I won't take time to tell you now, but I'm just fine. Any chance you, Paul, and Sari could meet me after work?"

"Yes!" she said without a moment's hesitation.

"So after work you will pick up Paul and Sari from school? Have you anything planned for the evening?" Harry quizzed.

"Yes and no. Whatever I was going to do would be pure nonsense to the kids if they knew they had an opportunity to see you."

"Wonderful. Come as soon as you change out of your work clothes." He gave her the name of a familiar market, stating he would meet them there.

If he thought *he* was happy, he should have heard the delightful dialogue at the Carson household. When she hung up, the children pummeled her with questions. She soon found out she had the answer to only two of their persistent inquiries.

"Harry is fine and I know where to meet him after school."

That had to suffice, for in her surprise and happiness at Harry's call, she had not thought to ask anything more.

The day passed very slowly for the children but altogether too fast for Harry. He hoped they would be pleased with his living arrangements.

"There he is, Mommy!" eagle-eyed Sari exclaimed.

"No, that's not him," Paul countered.

Harry's clothes looked much different from when they last saw him. He was standing very upright and without a cane. He saw their van and waved. Paul nearly jumped out before the car stopped and gave him an enormous bear hug. Sari, right on his heels, followed suit. Kathy approached more slowly, but she, too, hugged him.

All were strangely quiet for a few moments. Sari was the first to speak. "How are you, Harry?"

"Hanging in there," then added, "like a hair in a biscuit."

"Yuk!" she said. "I don't have hair in my biscuits."

They all chuckled as they entered the van, and Harry gave directions.

"I've missed you so much," Sari said as she leaned from behind and placed an arm across his shoulders. This small act never ceased to cause Harry to choke up.

"I have missed you too. Where did you go?" was Paul's question.

"Are you feeling all right?" asked Kathy.

"Tell us how you got away from the nursing home," urged Sari, who wanted details.

He was so very grateful for this loving and caring family. *Just think of what these children's father is missing*, he thought. He then proceeded to relate the story of his activities since he had last seen them.

"God has been so good to me. Had I told you on the telephone, you would not have believed me, so I have to let you experience it for yourself.

"That's Mrs. Grimbolt's residence," he pointed to a beautiful old house with an immaculate yard. The very first day I walked the streets wondering what would happen next, I came upon an old lady who was having trouble starting her lawn mower. I stopped to help her, and she put me to work."

He told them of the events leading up to his meeting Mrs. Grimbolt, her kindness, and of her disabilities brought on by the aging process. All along the street, both kids were oohing and aahing at the fancy houses and beautifully kept yards and giant old trees protected by aristocratic-looking fences. By the time he got to tell about Lillian, he said, "Turn into this drive."

"What do you mean?" Kathy said and kept driving.

"Stop! Back up."

Kathy shot him a questioning look but complied. She backed up and carefully nosed the vehicle into the drive. The kids were wide-eyed. He flicked his remote control and the big iron gates slowly opened. Harry watched the children. They had not blinked for seemed like minutes. Kathy stopped the van inside the gate while the children watched it close behind them. They silently peered about.

"Breathtaking, isn't it?" Harry said.

"Yes," they quietly chorused.

Questioning now began in earnest. It was more than he could answer all at once, so he said, "Let's first pull around to the back of the mansion."

He asked Kathy to stop in front of his house, instructing her to park beside the Toyota pickup.

"Nice house," Paul observed.

"Come inside. I want you to meet its tenant."

Kathy wondered why he had a key when he stepped to the door, turned the key in the lock, and ushered them in. She peered around him, looking for someone inside, when he spread his arms and said, "Meet the tenant."

Kathy had been getting altogether too many cerebral shocks from Harry's recent escapades. She sank speechless into a nearby chair while the kids were told to feel free to look around.

"Harry, talk to me! I'm dizzy trying to make heads and tails out of this … this … whatever! Start from when you left the nursing home."

"I'll tell all that and more, but please indulge me one more thing. You wait here just a few minutes. Come when I call you, OK?"

At her nod he left and was joined in the kitchen by Paul and Sari. All Kathy could hear was the noise of diligent activity, but the loudest of all was coming from two very excited and happy children. Occasionally, wedged in between the children's excitement, she could distinguish Harry's clear baritone voice. Those kids adored that man. He was fulfilling a need that their own father would not provide.

Their father—it has been years since he stopped inquiring about us. He hurt us all but mostly the children. They have missed having a father. It is that time in life when a dad should be talking to his son about becoming a man.

"Come here, Mom!" the children shouted, interrupting her pensive mood.

"No, wait," cried Paul. He had caught the mood for lightheartedness and fun. "Stay where you are, Mother, I'll come and get you." On the way past the refrigerator, he grabbed a dish towel hanging from the door handle. "Mom, I want to tie this around your head so you can't see. I'll lead you." Obediently she consented. All was quiet to where she was being taken. Paul stopped her and said, "Close your eyes while I take off the blindfold. Don't open them until we say to."

"Open your eyes," Harry said softly. Before she had her eyes completely focused, she heard singing:

"A happy birthday to you,
A happy birthday to you.
Every day of the year,
May you feel Jesus near.
A happy birthday to you,

A happy birthday to you,

The best that you ever knew!"

She stood gazing at the scene before her, only faintly hearing the chorus of voices around her. This was too much. Her hands flew to her chest, then to her eyes, then one at her neck and the other to her eyes. She was overcome with emotion. Over the years the children tried in their simple way to make something of her birthday, and while she always appreciated it, she could not think of a birthday more meaningful than this one. The children saw her astonishment turn to embarrassment and rushed to her side to comfort and hug her. She tried hugging them back, but she needed both hands to stay the flow of emotion.

Harry fetched a box of tissues. He was hoping the tears were of joy and not anger. He did not have long to wait, for he suddenly felt Kathy's arms surround his neck while she leaned against him trying to quiet sobs of joy. Paul and Sari had now encircled them both with outstretched arms.

Kathy felt Harry's tender embrace, savored it for a moment, and gently pulled away.

"Are you happy, Mom?" Sari inquired, misty eyed.

"Did we surprise you?" Paul wanted to know.

"I am speechless and completely overwhelmed. That includes being happy and surprised."

This is what she saw, a table set for four, with flickering candlelight, a white lace tablecloth, attractive china, and properly placed silverware on top of smoothly pressed and neatly folded cloth napkins. Crystal goblets were filled with sparkling grape juice.

Harry cleared his throat and said, "Please be seated."

He stood behind Sari's chair, much to her liking, and seated her.

Paul, seeing what was happening, tried to do the same for his mother. Perhaps not too gracefully, Harry noted, but good for a beginner. Interestingly, good manners beget good manners. They joined hands and Harry prayed. "Our loving Father in Heaven. My heart is filled and overflowing with the goodness You have shown to me. Please bless Kathy, Paul, and Sari, without whom I would never have recovered to this point." He paused, struggling with an obstruction in his throat. "I am thankful for You, my Creator and Savior, and for providing friendship and this food. Amen."

Sounds of laughter and cheerful conversation followed the prayer, making for a very pleasant start to the evening.

Knowing everyone was vegetarian, Harry had taken special care to please. He prepared a tossed green salad, mashed potatoes (he tried Sari's recipe), steamed broccoli, peas, corn, and a relish tray consisting of radishes, sliced cucumbers, both black and green olives, and carrots, all on a bed of lettuce.

During the meal, around mouths full of delicious food, they asked a multitude of questions, all of which he tried to answer with as much detail. He told of leaving the nursing home the first day, how he felt compelled to return when he did not know where to spend the night.

"You could have stayed in my room," Paul said.

"Yes," Kathy agreed, and continued, "I heard about the reincarnation of Old Sam." She related the story from her perspective for the children. "There is still talk about it," she laughed. "I thought I had answers to their questions but did not let on."

"Thank you," Harry said. The children wanted to know in detail about Harry sleeping in Old Sam's bed and eating his food after Sam had died. They laughed and laughed until their bellies ached from mental visions they each conjured up about a dead man eating food, making his bed and then suddenly disappearing.

Harry told about Mrs. Grimbolt's frustration with her lawnmower and not being able to care for her landscaping. He told them of his night at the airport.

"Mrs. Grimbolt introduced me to Lady McKenzie, who wanted a maintenance supervisor. I do not have to do any physical work, just supervise. She said I could still help Mrs. Grimbolt and do whatever I wanted, as long as McKenzie Manor continued to be a showcase. And here we are."

While Harry was talking with the children, Kathy cleared the table and stacked the dishes. Harry insisted on leaving the dishes to be washed later because he had other plans for them just now.

"Let's take a walk."

"Show me your maintenance shop," Paul pleaded.

"I want to see the horses," Sari chirped.

"Perhaps we should let Harry lead the way," advised Kathy.

Harry showed them many things about the place. He had not seen the estate in its entirety himself yet.

"Hello there," said a voice from behind.

Turning, Harry said, "Hello, Mrs. McKenzie, I'm showing some friends around."

"Please feel free to do so." She came over to get a closer look at his friends, and introductions were made. "Call me Lillian; everybody does."

Sari said, "You have a beautiful palace. Are you a queen or something?"

Mrs. McKenzie laughed. "My husband treated me like one, and Harry is making the place fit for the Queen of England's summer castle."

"Do you know the Queen of England?" asked Sari.

"No, but would you like to see my pal— ... home?"

"Oh, Queen Lillian, may I?" Sari was delighted and pressed her little hand into Lillian's.

"I see that you two are heading toward the gardens. So, Paul and Sari, you come along with me." She took a hand of each child and over her shoulder spoke to Kathy, "Harry can show you my house later."

"She seems like a really nice older lady," Kathy observed.

Hmmm … Did she stress "older," or was it my imagination? Harry wondered.

"Yes, but I think she is very lonesome. The cook told me Lillian had two babies, but both died in infancy."

They had approached a garden of rare varieties of roses.

"That's a gorgeous French Lace," Kathy exclaimed and pointed to a beautiful, eye-catching, yellow-tinged white flower. "And there's a most fragrant red rose."

"I didn't know you were so familiar with roses."

"That's an American Beauty, and there's a Mister Lincoln," she finished.

"These are supposed to be rare, so I thought I was going to tell you something new and interesting," he frowned.

"These are indeed unusual. I love them, and some have a heavenly fragrance like this." She was back at the French Lace.

"When it is practical, I want to make a flower garden and have bunches of roses."

"Ouch!" she cried as she reached to pull a stem closer.

"Let me see that." He quickly pulled out a handkerchief and wrapped it around her pricked finger.

"Sorry, you need to be careful with the thorns."

Only after arriving at the carnation enclosure did he realize he was still holding the handkerchief to her pricked pinky. They simultaneously self-consciously jerked apart, each showing expressions of surprise yet tenderness. In this moment of frustration, he totally forgot the carnation enclosure and was standing in front of a giant elm. Opening his mouth to give some deep discourse on flowers, he looked first at the elm, then at Kathy, and they both burst into laughter.

"What are you two giggling about?" Paul said as he came around the shrubs to see his mother and Harry enjoying a good laugh.

"Harry was expounding on the culture and habits of carnations," Kathy said, still chuckling. Paul looked at the tree and then back to the carnation garden in the distance and could not quite put the two together as they all stood looking up into the elm.

"Where's your sister?"

"You know old question box. She won't run out till next week."

"I'd better go rescue Mrs. McKenzie."

"I left because they were playing with dolls," Paul said, sounding bored and uninterested. "Where's the tool shop?"

"Really, Sari doesn't know when to stop," reminded Kathy. "I'll go and relieve Mrs. McKenzie.

"All right, come this way. It's a short cut. We will stop at the manor, and then Paul and I will proceed to the garage."

Harry led them through arbors loaded with delicious-looking grapes. Paul stopped for a sample but caught up as they approached the door of the house. Inside the mansion they could hear happy sounds from two contented girls, one considerably older chronologically but young in spirit, dressing up dolls and dialoguing in a make-believe world.

"Queen Lillian and I are playing dolls," Sari said when she heard the others enter.

"I see, and beautiful dolls they are. These are exquisite specimens," Kathy said as she admired the collection.

"My husband and I did a lot of traveling for his businesses, and I purchased at least one in every country and culture we visited."

"I especially love this one, Mommy. See the long black hair, the pretty blue eyes—and isn't the dress gorgeous?"

"She is a beauty!"

During this conversation Paul was in the background wrinkling his nose to no one in particular. Harry caught the message, nudged Paul, and nodded toward the door.

"I hope you don't mind my indulging your daughter. She is such a pleasant child. A breath of fresh air, really. I haven't taken the dolls from their display cases in ages. Don't know when I have felt so young as I do now being with you, Sari," she said.

"Thank you very much for your kind hospitality," Kathy said. "I can see Sari has certainly enjoyed getting to know you."

"Will you come visit me and my dolls, Queen Lillian?" asked Sari.

Lillian, turned, picked up the doll Sari had admired, and gently placed it in her arms, saying, "Take Irena home with you. I'll visit her when I come to see you." Sari stretched to give Lillian a hug around her neck and a kiss on her cheek. The older woman brushed at something in her eyes.

"Thank you! I'll take good care of her."

"I know you will, dear."

Lillian rescued Kathy, not knowing exactly what to say. "You know, I have no one to give my things to when I die. I think your visit has given me an idea. Harry must be an angel to have brought me so much happiness in such a short time."

"We'd better be going."

"Thank you, Lillian, and goodbye. We'll arrange for your visit soon," Kathy said.

Kathy, along with Sari, who was hugging Irena, followed a path that seemed to identify with the directions Mrs. McKenzie gave her. The guys had gone on to the maintenance building, but the girls caught them before they reached it.

Harry pointed out things of interest as they made their way to the tool shop. They passed a gazebo where on very special occasions a band or ensemble played at parties for select groups of friends and acquaintances.

Past a peacock enclosure, they finally came to the tool shop. Harry turned the key and opened the door. Inside, Paul was soon in his element. He saw a complete wood working section, a fabricating area, and a mechanics work place. Each work zone was fully equipped. There were shelves of nuts, bolts, nails, screws, and welding rods, stacks of lumber neatly organized amongst a myriad of other materials. Kathy's appraisal was that it resembled a small home improvement store. Harry explained some of the more sophisticated machinery, but Paul already knew how most of it worked.

Reading the body language of the girls in the group and thus discerning the beginnings of boredom, Harry said, "Paul, come along to my house in ten minutes. Do you think you can find it? Look around all you want and turn the lights off, and close and lock the door when you leave, OK? I've got something more to do at the house." Harry thought Paul understood the instructions but was more convinced when he paused, and the silence made Paul look up.

"Yes, all right. Ten minutes, " Paul confirmed.

"Take a seat at the bar," Harry said as he began to putter in the kitchen. Sari took Irena into the living room.

"Now, what are you doing?" Kathy questioned.

"You can help me. We didn't have dessert, if you recall. Everyone was too full to have it at dinner time, so I thought we could have it now," answered Harry.

He produced some biscuits he had tried to make. They were slightly burned and probably pretty durable, judging from the sounds they made when falling on the counter top. Paul entered as Harry put the finishing touches of whipped cream on the strawberry-covered biscuits. He stuck a candle in each one and called for Sari. They sang the birthday song again.

"It is traditional to have a birthday cake, you know, so I made a small one for you take home."

All had a good time, and each said so as they filed out and into the van for the ride home. Harry felt good about being on the giving end for a change. *Every friendship has to share a give-and-take relationship*, he thought. For months he had been incapable of doing anything nice for anyone, especially for those he called friends. He entered his house, quickly washed the dessert dishes, and fell into bed. He was very tired, but he had a good feeling about himself and the evening's events.

Chapter Seventeen

The next week Harry responded to an urgent call from Mrs. Grimbolt, who said she needed his advice. She had been giving some thought to his suggestion about a riding lawn mower.

"Will you help me select a good one?"

She was such a dear lady. She looked so helpless now peering up into his face.

"Certainly. When shall we shop?"

"Right now!"

"Right now?"

"Yes, my arthritis is tolerable for the moment."

He sank into the soft plush leather seat of the Lincoln, and they were off. They stopped at three places but finally decided to go back to the first store to make the purchase.

You drive home, Harry."

Oh, no! He was hoping she would not ask. He started toward the driver's side, then drew back saying, "I don't have my operator's license with me."

He wondered if she ever questioned why he always arrived at her place on a bicycle. His driver's license should arrive in the mail any day now. She had several errands to run, so by the time they arrived home, the newly purchased riding lawnmower had already been delivered and was parked in her driveway.

Harry helped her climb onto the seat, explained each control, shifted it into a low gear, and instructed her to test drive it around the yard a few times in order to gain confidence. She did so and thought she was ready to mow. He then showed her how to engage the mower deck and walked behind while she circled several times around the big yard. He watched her from the shade of a giant oak tree.

Not yet finished, she stopped the machine, slowly got off, and hobbled toward him. He could see her arthritis was bothering her now.

"Would you mind finishing the job? My bones are feeling old and stiff." She shuffled into the house without further comment, and he finished the mowing. After parking the machine in the shed, he found Mrs. Grimbolt on the sun porch waiting for him with a glass of cool Guava punch.

"You are right, that is a lot easier and faster than that old push thing. I don't know how much longer I can work in my yard," she said sadly.

"God never allows more than we can handle if we choose His help," Harry offered, venturing into an uncharted subject with her.

"What do you mean? I don't know that I have ever heard such a thing."

"I mean, God knows our strengths, our weaknesses, and our infirmities. He offers to help fortify our strengths and sustains us in our limitations, thereby enriching our lives and those around us. While that may be primarily a spiritual concept, He made us and understands both our mental and physical bodies as well. Do you know God?" That was a question she had never been asked and was slow in answering.

"If you mean, do I go to church, the answer is, yes." After a slight hesitation, she meekly added, "usually."

"Do you know God?" he asked her again.

"You're making this hard for me, Harry, but I would like to talk about it. My pastor has never asked me that question."

Harry continued, "I have had an experience through which I would not have successfully passed had God not been with me and blessed me. During this encounter I had a lot of time to ponder life and its meaning. I realized I had strayed away from God. Through talking with Him and thinking about His goodness, I was impressed to follow Him who knows the end from the beginning. Even though He has done miraculous things in my life, I am committed to Him no matter what may happen. He has had thousands of years of experience, and I have developed a complete trust in Him.

"As I understand it, when God made Adam and Eve, He walked and talked with them just as you and I are doing right now. They had a familiar or personal friendship with their Maker. They told Him their concerns and problems. He told them how to solve them. They got sick and He instructed them how to care for themselves. They thanked Him for the wonderful ways in which He showed His care and love for them. He was very personal to our first parents, and He wants to be the same with us. The way I see it, Mrs. Grimbolt, people move away from Him. He doesn't go anywhere. He is by our side just waiting for us. I believe He still wants us to walk and talk with Him. He hasn't promised us a life without pain and challenges, but He has assured us He will help with every difficulty we face.

"With the wonderful gardenlike atmosphere you have here, this is a good place to meet with Him anytime you want to right here among the flowers and trees, just as He did with Adam and Eve. The Bible says they walked and talked with Him in the cool of the evening."

Tears moistened her kind, gentle doe eyes, and slipped down through the lines of her wrinkled cheeks, but she let them flow freely.

"You are right. Thank you for your candidness. I knew about God as a child but … excuse me, I believe I'll take a walk in the garden," and she hobbled away. "Goodbye and thank you."

Several more weeks passed. Life fell into a comfortable routine for Harry. His health was returning surprisingly well. He attended church on weekends, where he usually saw Kathy, Paul, and Sari. Sometimes he stayed for fellowship dinner—always when Paul or Sari, or both, prompted him to do so. He enjoyed a rather relaxed work schedule through the week that included mowing Mrs. Grimbolt's lawn and supervising Mrs. McKenzie's maintenance crew. He exercised regularly and ate healthfully. He saw a doctor regularly during the first six months but was soon pronounced physically and mentally fit, was dismissed but instructed to schedule biannual visits, and was advised to call at the first symptom of trouble.

Sometimes he bicycled just for the exercise, but this morning he chose to walk. He came upon a car lot he often passed by, but today as he approached, he observed a man washing cars. He did not remember seeing him on previous jaunts. The man's angry, jerky actions indicated he was not happy about something. He yanked the hose and slopped more soapy water on himself than on the cars. All the time his mouth issued a stream of unintelligible gibberish.

Harry stopped still to avoid an uncontrolled spray of water crossing his path, then detoured into the street. He walked onto the lot, went behind an already washed vehicle where he would be semi-protected from errant sprays of water, and nodded to the car washer, who did not acknowledge him. A few moments passed as Harry observed the man's attitude. "Mr. Washer Man" occasionally glanced his way and, seeing that the visitor was not going away, grunted and forced a smile that did not reach his eyes.

"Yes?" he grumbled. "You'se wanna buy a car?"

Harry smiled.

"Yo'se want'a buy a car 'er somthin?" He asked again, a little louder. This man looked and acted Irish. Perhaps he had a kinship to Harry's ancestors. He thought he would give him a test.

"Sure, 'n' wouldn't I be a needin' one now. Me legs culd get a proper rest."

"Aye, 'an are ye an Emerald Islander, 'er what?" He advanced, held out a hand the size of a baseball mitt, and barked, "Michael O'Brien at cher service. People call me Mike."

"Harry Tucker," he introduced himself as Mike pumped his hand in a bear claw. I pass your lot several times a week, but I haven't seen you before. You are not the usual car washer."

"Of course you don't. I don't wash cars! I'm the owner!" he exploded. "I'm supposed to sell 'em."

"You keep your cars looking very nice. How often are they cleaned?"

"Not often enough. I've seen you. You'se sometimes ride a bicycle, sometimes walk, right?"

"That's me."

"Can't keep a boy aroun' long 'nuff to do it 'cept two, maybe three times, and he's off makin' more money somewheres else."

While they talked, Harry recognized an opportunity and finally, to get a word in blurted, "I'll contract with you to take care of your cars." Seemed like he had to speak whether or not Mike was talking if he wanted to get a word in.

"Yer'll what?"

"I'll take care of the cars for you."

"Come in and we'll talk about it."

Mike was the owner of this new and used car establishment and was out cleaning the cars himself! Harry could not believe it and told Michael O' Brien so.

"Isn't your time more valuable than to spend it washing cars?" Mike interrupted. Not indicating he had heard, he said, "It takes a lot of time and energy to keep those cars sparklin' clean. Ya' know, first impression's the best and longest lastin'."

"I'll take care of them for you," Harry repeated, louder this time.

"If you think you can keep 'em clean and shining, I'll try ya' out."

Harry attempted a second time to be heard. "How often should they be washed?"

"I'll tell you what I 'spect and you tell me if you can deliver."

They settled on a schedule and Harry said goodbye, already wondering how he would manage such a time-consuming menial job. His overactive analytical mind was already processing the problem, and a plan was taking shape in his brain. It brought a smile to his face. He felt so good that he jogged partway home, not an easy thing to do with a lame leg.

Two days later Mr. O'Brien looked out over his extensive lot filled with costly vehicles to see kids rushing up and down the shiny rows, their arms pistoning and hands flying all over his brand new cars.

"What the!" Thinking a gang of hoodlums had descended looking to do harm, he barged out the door, nearly knocking Harry off his feet, and barked like a drill sergeant. "Get them scoundrels out'a here," he commanded in no uncertain terms. His lack of good diction did not interfere with either his voice volume, or his quantity or quality of words. Language to make one's mother blush was thrown in for good measure.

"Can't do that," Harry said calmly.

"What're those ragamuffins doin' to my cars?" he shouted.

Unruffled, Harry said, "Washing them. Doing a good job, too."

"Get 'em out'a here! Get 'em out'a here NOW! Hear me, Harry? I said NOW and I'll hold you personally 'sponsible for any damage done to 'em cars," he roared.

A car door slammed, and as he turned, trying to be cool, anticipating a perspective customer, he heard, "Hello, Mr. O'Brien."

"Hello, to you, Mrs. Carson," syrup in his voice. Your new van is meeting your expectations, I trust?"

"Oh, yes, I'm thankful for your interest in helping me select just the right auto. I transported these kids in it today to wash your cars, and they are doing a superb job of it, don't you think? It does my heart good to see a man of your position and responsibility place such confidence in young people. Certainly, the community will know about this."

Mike, distracted by this woman who was his customer, had cooled a degree or two, just enough to pretend control, and could now more objectively observe the work going on.

"Well, er, ah, why maybe … per'aps so. That is Harry's responsibility." As he watched the boys and girls carefully wash and chamois dry, then wash the windows inside and out, he stood in awe observing a well-behaved army of well-disciplined youth. He scratched his head, still showing obvious beads of sweat cascading down reddened cheeks, and smiled at Kathy.

His brisk behavior gradually gave way to near calmness as he said, "Well, all right this time, but … where's Harry? I wanna talk at em!" Then Smitty, his sales manager, who was beckoning, waving a telephone, interrupted him.

The second time the kids showed up, Mike was not there, but all went well. This age group of kids from Paul's church had accepted the challenge to build a jungle chapel in Africa, and they were looking for and willing to do odd jobs to raise the money. They were a good group of kids from hard-working families with parents who set high Christian standards in behavior and example.

Paul's friends were boys and girls who called themselves "The HK Club," HK meaning "His Kids." They had been at their car-washing job for about a month. Mike O'Brien had insisted that they could not work past the probation period. Harry was in Mike's office now discussing the contract.

"The kids have appreciated you letting them wash cars, but they haven't heard if you're happy with them or not, so they are looking for something else. They like you and they don't want to offend you if you think they are doing a poor job."

"They what?" Mike interrupted. He heard only the part about them looking for something else. He slammed his fist on the desk and jumped out of his chair, sending it ricocheting to the wall.

"They can't do that! They're doin' the best job I've ever had. They can't jus' walk away. We got a contract Harry, or have you fergot?"

"You gave thirty days' probation, and the contract is up in a couple of days," Harry reminded him, smiling behind his hand.

"I'm satisfied, and customers comment on the nice 'pearance of clean cars. I don' wan' 'em to leave me," he passionately pleaded.

Harry knew that Mike was not all huff and puff, but his contrition pleasantly surprised him.

"Then you need to tell them. People like to be appreciated, especially kids, you know. They need approval and encouragement."

"I have a problem saying thanks," Mike solemnly mumbled.

"I've noticed," Harry remarked. Mike winced at the truthfulness.

"You get more out of a person from a pat on the back than from a raise in salary or shouting criticism. People like to feel they're part of the team, like to feel they're contributing, and like to be told so."

Harry was not sure where his comments would take him. But he knew Mike was an honest man. Harry's fears were soon put to rest.

Mike quieted. "Yeah, I need help in 'at department a'right. I've noticed how you get a lot out'a 'em kids. You get on 'em when they need to do better and they still like ya. Wanna help me?"

Surprised, but happy that this very proud, self-reliant man asked for help, Harry said, "It's simple, really. Begin right now. Don't put it off. Determine that you are going to encourage at least one person each day with some act of kindness, whether it's a smile, a thank you, a pat on the back, a high five, or a minute or two of quality time spent one on one. You might start with someone in your family, like your wife. Women like flowers, candy, and a special night out with just the two of you. Just think of how you would like someone to treat you and you do it to him or her."

"Like the golden rule, eh?"

"It hasn't been improved upon," Harry smiled.

"Tell 'ose kids of yours they can't leave me, and if they do, I won't donate enough for a complete jungle chapel. How much for one anyway?"

"A couple hundred dollars, I presume."

"I'll give for one. No, make it two."

"That's very generous of you. Tell you what. The kids will be here this afternoon after school. You can tell them yourself." He left before Mike could raise an argument.

That afternoon after the kids completed their car cleaning assignment, Mike called them into the conference room where he conducted staff meetings with his sales force. The children sat in large chairs around a big table. They saw walls covered with sales charts, incentive schedules, pictures of new cars, and posters of race cars and their famous drivers. They were quiet and sober, wondering what Mr. O'Brien wanted to say to them. They had never been in this room before. He sounded gruff when he called for them to come in.

Previously, Harry had always dealt with Mike. They wondered where he was now. The kids knew they were on probation, and though they felt they did a good job, Mike was always grumbling about something and kept an eagle eye on them when he was on the lot.

The door opened abruptly and Mike stomped in. All the kids at once stood to attention like soldiers when their commanding officer enters. Mike smiled to himself. These were good kids, he thought, and polite, too. Harry had been right from the beginning.

"Sit down!" It was hard for him to speak softly. "Did Harry tell ya' what I wan'ed ta say ta ya?"

"No, sir," they timidly answered.

"This here car wash'en thing you're doin' …" he let the impact linger a moment, "this is serious business. I told yer Harry it's a man's job. But he don't listen. I need 'em cars looking spotless ya' know. Have any of you'se ever gone car shoppin' wid yer parents?" There were several nods and a few timidly raised hands. "Would ja like to buy a dirty new car?"

The children were looking depressed, and their countenances faded. This was Mike's tactic with his sales people when they lagged behind schedule. The children seemed to fade at his unswerving stare into their faces. But he saw clean, innocent, honest expressions on guiltless faces. He grunted to himself. They didn't deserve this kind of treatment. In the recesses of his mind, he heard Harry's pep talk. He cleared his throat and gave a steely stare.

This was it, the children thought. In one month's time they had earned almost enough for a jungle chapel to be constructed in Africa. For about an average day's pay, a simple thatched roof building with open sides could be built. All they needed was something to protect them from the rain and hot sun. The children had been very excited about this project. They actually were trying to raise enough money for two chapels. Every meeting they had with Harry, they would look at a picture of the type of chapel they were working to build. A lot of enthusiasm had been generated.

Mike was speaking again, "I've put my trust in Harry and you'uns to keep my cars clean and 'spectable lookin' and what do I get? WHAT DO I GET?" he shouted.

He paused as he glanced around at each face. "What do YOU get?" His voice boomed this time. He paused again, looked around the room full of kids, and, with an unaccustomed smile in his eyes, said, "I get the best job I've ever had done and YOU'SE get a donation for two jungle chapels besides the one you're working on!"

Judging from the silence in the room, Mike thought they had not understood him. Not being a quiet person himself, he could not take the extended quiet any longer and was ready to say something when the room exploded. He was nearly knocked off his feet but quickly sat down to maintain balance as the kids cheered. The boys gave him high fives and the girls gave hugs. He was inundated with small arms and children's voices all talking and thanking him at the same time. For once he was at a loss for words and felt something like an obstruction in his throat that almost did not respond to persistent throat clearing and swallowing before the effect reached his eyes.

His hand finally found the intercom, and while Suzie, his secretary, did not understand the words he was speaking because of the background noise, she knew it was her cue.

Cookies, hot chocolate, and a large basket of fruit was brought in, and the noise of happy children only slightly subsided as they slurped and munched the treats. All around the room between sounds of chewing and lip smacking, the kids were saying things like "You're the greatest!" and "Thank you, Mr. O'Brien. I'm going to tell my dad to buy a car from you, and I'll buy one too when I'm old enough! God bless you!"

The good feeling Mike was enjoying was foreign to him. He had planted a seed of kindness Harry had told him about—the results of which made him want to raise a big garden of kindness. The fruit was delicious.

Over the weeks Harry had become well acquainted with Smitty, Mike's new car sales manager. One day while they were talking, a telephone call came for Smitty. When he hung up, he looked stressed and acted agitated.

"Did that call upset you as much as it looks on your face?"

"There's a lot of pressure in the car business. One of the continuing problems I face is getting vehicles. Trucks deliver autos from a central distribution point, to be sure, but we always need single units from other dealerships with whom we constantly trade. We try to maintain 300 units on the lot, but there's always a customer who wants something specific, and we go to the extreme trying to satisfy them."

"So what's the problem?" Harry asked.

Exasperated, Smitty said, "The problem is getting reliable drivers to transport vehicles. No. Let me rephrase that. The problem is getting drivers! Right now I need a car from just across town and I have no one to drive it here."

"Seems simple enough. Sounds like an easy job to me. I'll go!"

"You? You can't do that!"

"Why not?" Harry asked.

Smitty could think of no good reason except that Harry needed to be bonded and to have his driving record researched.

Harry's business skills were being massaged. He missed his clinical laboratory services. He was a natural promoter and sensed that Smitty's problem could easily be solved. His mind was already putting together a small business venture that would mutually benefit both of them.

Chapter Eighteen

Paul looked up from the workbench in his garage and saw a block-long black limousine slow and finally stop in front of his house. He hastened to the back door, calling, "Mom, the Reader's Digest Sweepstakes car just stopped in front of our house! Did you win?"

"Son, you know I don't waste my time and money on things like that. That's probably Lillian McKenzie coming for a visit and sup- … dinner. Would you let her in, please?"

Paul held up his dirty hands.

"Sari," Kathy called, "please go to the door. Queen Lillian has arrived."

Kathy liked the title Sari gave to this nice lady. Sari let Lillian in, and soon Kathy joined them in the living room. Paul went back to his project.

"Mom, can I take Queen Lillian to my room?"

"Whenever are you going to stop calling me Queen Lillian, child? Everyone just calls me Lillian."

"Yes, ma'am."

While Kathy finished dinner preparations, Sari had Lillian all to herself in her room. Lillian was a good playmate.

Sari asked. "Why don't you have children? Seems that you like them."

"I had two, but they died a few days after birth. Charles, my husband, was disappointed, and we thought of adoption, but he traveled so much that it was an inconvenient time to have children."

"I'm glad my mom doesn't think I'm inconvenient," Sari said while busily redressing a doll for a dolly nap.

"If I had children, I'd want them just like you and your brother."

"That's so nice of you to say, but he is a boy, you know."

She smiled and said, "Yes, I've noticed," then added, "I mean it. Do you miss your father?"

"I never knew him, and I don't remember ever seeing him, except in a photograph.

Mom told us about him once, and we would talk more, but there is nothing to talk about. I guess he didn't want us. If I could choose a father, he would be Harry."

Lillian's eyes shot upward. "Harry?" Lillian's interest was piqued.

"Yes, I know he loves me. He's a very nice man, you know. He and Paul work together sometimes, and Paul loves him too. He told me so one time."

Lillian would not pry, of course. But she referred to her interest in such matters as "investigating."

"Paul built a ZYCLE for Harry," Sari said.

"What on earth is a ZYCLE?"

"It's a special exercise machine." Sari was more intent on getting her 'baby' to sleep than on the conversation.

"Exercise?" Lillian gently pried.

"When mommy first saw him, he was unconscious and unable to move. A stroke, they called it. Harry was very sick, you know."

After a quick glance at the door, Lillian lowered her voice just a little and said, "No, I don't, tell me about it."

Sari shared in great detail all she knew about Harry's stroke and the loss of his business as a result of the dealings of a dishonest attorney and a money-hungry son. She also told of her first meeting with him when she and her school visited the nursing home.

Not all of this information was new to Lillian. But it did confirm rumors of a very mysterious man.

"By using Paul's ZYCLE, he got the exercise he needed when insurance wouldn't pay for rehabilitation treatments. He even slept in Old Sam's bed the night he died, ate his food, and then left the nursing home. The nurse thought Old Sam had been resurrected, then raptured," Sari laughed. Lillian did not quite understand all of this but chuckled at the humor Sari saw. "Harry should tell you about it. It's funnier coming from him."

It was of particular interest to Lillian to hear about Sari's mother's involvement in the case.

"Did your mother give Harry physical therapy?"

"Yes, but only for a little while. His son didn't think it was helping, didn't want to spend the money, and stopped treatments when Harry did not get better. Mommy didn't want to give up because he was so young and she thought he would heal, so she gave him exercises he could do on his own. She helped when she could. Has Jesus ever healed you?" Sari's question snapped Lillian out of her musings.

"What do you mean, child?"

"Sometimes Jesus heals sickness. Have you ever been sick?"

"Yes."

"Did Jesus heal you?"

"I, I don't know," she answered haltingly.

"I suppose He did. He made our bodies, so He knows how to fix them, right?"

"You know a lot about the Bible, don't you?" Lillian tried to turn the attention away from herself.

"I know Jesus is my friend. And I know He is your friend, too."

"How did you learn so much about spiritual things?"

"From my mom, my church, and school. Would you like to go with me to church?" Sari was looking directly into Queen Lillian's eyes.

The honest, trusting, almost pleading eyes of the child could not be denied. From somewhere deep within, perhaps caused by Lillian's unsatisfied yearning, certainly from a repressed, long-ignored need, came a barely audible "yes."

Had Sari been looking into Lillian's eyes at this moment, she would have seen a mixture of sadness, happiness, the formation of tears, and an unstoppable growing love for this child.

"Dinner is ready," called Kathy as she came down the hall to Sari's room. She entered the doorway just as Sari completed diapering her 'baby.' Lillian stood with her back to Sari and sideways to Kathy. Sari went to wash her hands, and Lillian turned toward Kathy, tears streaming down her aged regal face. Kathy stepped to her and embraced the now silently sobbing older woman.

"Is something wrong, Lillian? Did Sari say something to offend you. She has a way of being too blunt sometimes. I'm sorry if she—"

"Oh, no," Lillian said, lifting her hand. "Yes, it was something she said but not in offense. May I talk with you after dinner?"

"Certainly. Use the bathroom in here," Kathy said, leading Lillian through her bedroom. "Is there something I can do?" Kathy's voice held compassion.

"Thank you, I'll be fine in a few minutes," she smiled as the tears now subsided.

By the time Paul finished scrubbing the last layer of dirt from his hands and face and changed clothes, they all entered the dining room about the same time. As Lillian approached the table, Paul stepped to the back of Lillian's chair and seated her. She smiled approvingly saying, "Thank you, Paul, it's been a long time since I was treated so gallantly by such a handsome young prince."

Lately Paul had started feeling self-conscious around ladies other than his mother and sister, and the warmth of his face revealed it. No one said anything, but as he glanced at Sari, he saw her humorous smirk.

They bowed their heads, and Paul offered a simple prayer. "Our Father in heaven, thank You for our home, this good food, and for the visit of our good friend Quee- … ah … Mrs. McK … Lillian. Amen."

Their dinner talk was pleasant and centered around school and upcoming activities. Paul noticed with obvious appreciation that Sari did not monopolize the conversation as they devoured their dinner of potato soup, a tossed green salad, and toasted garlic bread.

"Delicious and a gastronomical delight," declared Lillian. "A gastro- what?"

Harry said something like that about my mashed potatoes," Sari said, chuckling.

"That means my stomach is happy and satisfied," said Lillian.

When the simple meal was over, Paul and Sari knew their responsibilities and, without being prompted, cleared the table and washed the dishes while Kathy and Lillian took cups of Jasmine tea and sat down under the spreading chestnut tree in the backyard. In size, the Carsons' house was like a wart on a bullfrog in comparison to the McKenzie mansion. But the McKenzie house had never exuded the home atmosphere she felt here. From under the chestnut tree, you could see both back and side fences. While Lillian McKenzie's presence in such humble surroundings would intimidate many, Kathy was not affected. She was secure with her own life and family. She was thankful for her two children and a place in which to raise them.

"I feel so comfortable with you and your children … such peace and serenity I don't have with my usual friends and associates. Why is that, Kathy?" Not waiting for her to answer, she continued, "It's because you're honest, sincere, and unpretentious. You are genuine and unassuming. What you are comes from within, and I like it! And I want it!" she exclaimed.

A little embarrassed but knowing Lillian would come back to this subject, Kathy shifted emphasis temporarily.

"My children think a lot of you. Especially Sari."

"She is a wonderful girl! I wish I had had a daughter just like Sari."

"Is Sari what you wanted to talk about?"

"That girl really gets to me. Every time I'm with her, I feel something akin to jealousy. I'm ashamed to say so, but that's the way it is."

"I'm sorry if Sari—"

"No, it's not what she does," Lillian interrupted. She seemed to have trouble going on. "It's … it's, oh, I don't know. Yes, I do know! It's what she is! She has character!" she finally exclaimed. "I'm a rich old woman not needing a thing money can buy, and I thought I had everything I would ever need until I met Harry, then you folks. Being with Sari, I finally figured it out."

"What is it, Lillian?" Kathy, asked intently. She then noticed why Lillian was hesitating. Momentarily, Lillian had to exert all of her efforts to quiet her sobs. She found a tissue, daubed at her eyes, and went on.

"Peace and happiness! These two things seem a part of your family the way expensive clothes are a part of me."

"Would you like to be at peace, Lillian?"

"More than anything!" she whimpered. "Even with all that I have, there are anxieties that haunt my mind. Doctors and medicines don't help. I've seen specialists all over the world, but I know the problem is not physical."

"I'll be happy to share my experience and recipe for happiness with you, if you like."

"Please, do!"

Kathy related happy as well as sad childhood days, school, dating and its challenges, professional school, and then marriage.

"Almost before the honeymoon was over, Tad was having an affair. He was sorry, of course. I forgave him and we started over again rebuilding trust in our relationship. Not a year had passed when I learned he was meeting his secretary on 'business trips.' I was pregnant with Paul, who I felt needed a father whatever the cost. When Tad found out I was pregnant, he stopped his cavorting and stayed near me, even through the delivery. I felt he had changed. He said he had, and I desperately wanted to believe him. I have always believed in God, even as a child, but children aren't put to spiritual tests the way adults are. I became pregnant again and by the time I delivered Sari, Tad was living with someone else."

Kathy cried as she relived horrible experiences. Lillian, too, cried.

"The hardest part was dealing with rejection and abandonment. I loved Tad with complete, pure, and undefiled love. I gave myself entirely to him, not just physically, but my attention and devotion. My sole focus was my husband. Looking back, it could have been easier, but I blamed not only Tad and others but also God as well as myself. My mother helped me see that God doesn't always take away the mountains and valleys of life, but He walks with us as we tread step by step through the desolate desert experiences. She reminded me of what Jesus told his friends when He was here on earth, and she quoted Bible texts like 'I will never leave you or forsake you' and 'Cast all your cares upon Him.' I can write these out for you if you would like me to."

Lillian nodded, still drying wet cheeks. "So I learned how to put my trust in the One who promised to help, and I have never been disappointed. I have experienced loneliness, despair, and an uncertain future. My heart aches with longing when I think of how much it would mean to me to have a husband and a good father for my children. God knew what lay ahead for me and gave me two wonderful children. 'He supplies all our needs' is another verse I have heavily relied on."

Paul brought the two women more hot water to refresh their tea, but sensing a serious conversation taking place, he quickly excused himself.

"God has helped bring contentment into my uncertain life, and He will do so for you, Lillian. Jesus said, 'Come to me all who are burdened and heavy laden, and I will give you rest.' It was the 'rest' that appealed to me. I was worried about what friends thought, worried about finances, worried about raising two babies by myself, about maintaining a happy home when all happiness had been dashed. My dear mother reminded me of that last text too. So, late one night when I was particularly sad and discouraged, with the world caving in around me, and I could think of no way out, I sank to my knees and gave all my burdens to the Lord. I told Him about my sadness, the feelings of rejection, problems with the lack of money, the loneliness, about the fear of raising two babies alone, and of my uncertainties about the future. Oh, I must have been on my knees most of the night pouring out my heart to Him. Then, the peace that started filling me was awesome. I can't describe it in human terms, but to experience it, is divine.

"Sometimes even now when I feel discouraged, I remember that experience with Jesus. It was like being baptized when you feel the water rising to your waist, then chest, arms, shoulders, finally covering your face and head. I went to my knees in despair and stayed there basking in contentment and a sense of peace I had never before known. As I related my problems, to my best Friend one by one, He took them, and I was released from all those negative feelings of hopelessness."

Lillian sat transfixed as she thought of her own perplexities of life. She moved not a muscle. Only her face expressed degrees of agony and hurt as Kathy related her experience.

"Lillian, it isn't as though I don't have worries, problems, or anxieties. You can well imagine the concerns I have with the children, let alone everything else. The promise 'I will be with you till the end of the earth' has become precious to me. I have also come to the conclusion that God has never failed in anything. So, as long as I'm with Him and He's with me, I'll be well taken care of."

Lillian did not want to say anything that might break the peace and serenity of the moment. Kathy saw she was deep in thought and remained silent. She could see that God's Spirit was working on her heart. Her countenance varied from darkness to a seemingly divine illumination, then clouded again until she finally displayed a look of contentment.

Finally, Lillian spoke. "I want this peace you talk about. I must have it!"

"It is something money cannot buy, but it is worth everything you have." Kathy slid to her knees, Lillian beside her. "Talk to God as you have talked to me. Tell Him everything." And Lillian did. Haltingly at first, sort of feeling her way as with a newfound friend, then like a rushing river she told God of her mistakes in life and of her feelings of emptiness, worthlessness, and loneliness. She ended with heartfelt praises that must have made the singing angels in heaven strike a higher note as a new believer in Jesus accepted eternal life.

The two women embraced for long moments. They had been talking for hours, but they hadn't noticed the passing time. Now composed, they entered the house arm in arm with tear-streaked faces but showing no embarrassment, only happiness. Lillian squeezed Sari and grabbed Paul before he shot out of arm's reach.

"I am the world's happiest woman!" she exclaimed. "I must thank you for it, Sari. I love you both," she said as she hugged them. Just as Paul thought he was going to be smothered, she released him. At the door she again held Kathy for a moment before reluctantly taking her leave.

Chapter Nineteen

"But, Mrs. McKenzie, I feel like I'm robbing you." With exasperation in his voice, Harry was trying to explain why he should be placed on a reduced salary or at least limited benefits. "Mickey is doing very well. I've trained him in every aspect of maintenance. He learns quickly and loves his work and has the respect of the other employees." He raced on trying to avoid interruption.

Lillian would have none of it. "I hired you to do a job, if you recall. I am more than satisfied because you have assumed the responsibility of taking care of managing the gardening and maintenance. It is one less burden for me to worry about. No, two. So if you're happy, I'm happy. The place looks the best it has in years. The money I'm paying you is immaterial."

"That's just the point. I'm being paid for full-time employment, but I spend a lot of time pursuing other ventures not remotely related to your maintenance," he said again for the third time.

"Are you looking for a raise?" she questioned, hiding a smile. She was enjoying his frustration but wondered where it would lead. She had to admire this man, for she knew more of him than she let on. She thought about what had transpired with him from the time they first met at Mrs. Grimbolt's place. He had appeared frail and shaky after only a few hours of work on her yard. It was evident he did good work and was a good manager. Certainly, she was happy with him. Lillian had been desperately searching for a responsible man to take charge of maintenance when her man of many years had become ill and had to retire.

She had secured Harry's employment before thoroughly checking into his background, something she had never done before and for which she was thoroughly reprimanded by her accountant and attorney. Perhaps she was failing in old age, but his look of honesty and evident ability convinced her. He had also offered to help Sadie. He fixed her lawn mower, chose an excellent riding lawn mower, and only after completing the yard work would he eat. He did not ask for money and objected when she offered it. She knew he certainly needed work, judging from those horrible mismatched clothes he wore.

Lillian's mind wandered with many thoughts. Oh, well, all in all the arrangements had worked out surprisingly well. As part of her "investigation," she had Harry's background searched, and when it came across her desk, she nearly hyperventilated. She'd had no clue as to his life before he came into hers. Now she learned he had been an entrepreneur and had owned a successful medical laboratory. Now look at him. He had organized her work and was responsible for a dozen or so other weekly landscaping assignments. He also supervised the car cleaning at Mike O'Brien's dealership by organizing Paul's friends to do the actual work. He had not only all these enterprises but now he was transporting new vehicles for Mike O'Brien. He instituted all these ventures in twelve months' time. He even had the kids known as the HK Club making homemade root beer and selling it along with popcorn at sporting events and church socials. Harry was excellent at delegating. It seemed there was no end to his skills.

The car transportation service was becoming too demanding for one person. To meet with the growing need for good automobile drivers, Harry met with the local senior citizens group and asked if there were responsible, diligent, extremely careful retirees who would be interested in part-time employment. He described in detail what the work would entail. He did not want any disillusioned employees. A larger number than he anticipated were eager to get off their backsides and commence with gainful employment. There was a long list of eager people waiting for an assignment.

How does he do it? Lillian wondered to herself. *My husband would certainly have loved to know a man with his abilities.*

"I have a distinct impression you are not listening to me," Harry interrupted her thoughts.

She glanced up from her chair, gave him an un-interpretable, slightly mischievous grin, and waved him off, saying, "I contracted with you to do a job. Whether or not it takes all day to do it is not my concern. I look at the results."

Harry had grown to respect and care for Lillian. He did not like the thought of taking advantage of anyone … rich elderly ladies included. After all, he had to live with himself. He was very conscientious about his dealings with all people. In fact, his conscience was nagging him at this very moment. Mrs. Grimbolt was visiting Lillian, and during pauses in their conversation, he felt this would be as good a time as any to clear his troubled mind, because what he needed to say involved them both, even though he was not yet finished talking about the salary Lillian was paying him. He recalled a time when he needed to supplement meager earnings as a young student in college. The training he had received to work as an emergency medical technician qualified him to do paramedical multi-physical exams for life insurance companies. To avoid being late for an appointment, he drove his overheated car several miles, causing severe motor damage. He paid dearly for car repairs, but he was conscientious in meeting his appointment.

"Please allow me to say something while both of you ladies are together. It does my heart good to see the way you care for each other. I think it's wonderful the way neighbors can be compatible to the point of checking on one another daily."

Mrs. McKenzie responded, "It's easy. Look around and observe older people. The older they get, the more in common they have."

Harry had to think about that for a while but finally had to agree. In the meantime he had something to say, and these ladies were making it hard for him.

He now had to come clean. He cleared his throat a couple of times, took a sip of the lemonade Lillian's servant had brought, and said, "I have a confession to make. I have escaped..."

At this, Mrs. Grimbolt's expression quickly turned from contentment to concern and anxiety, while Lillian's face displayed... what was it? A smile? He could see he must hasten and added quickly, "No, I'm not an escaped convict as I must have looked when first meeting you ladies, but ... perhaps I should start from the beginning. Do you mind? I'll hurry."

"No! Please take your time, young man," Lillian answered to both comments. Mrs. Grimbolt still sat with her mouth open.

Lillian's lips were slightly curled for either a verbal attack or a joke.

"I have been what some people would call very successful in the health care profession. By education, I am a medical technologist. I owned and operated a very large clinical medical laboratory. Mrs. Gimbolt had not moved in her rocking chair, and Lillian sat relaxed, knowing this part about Harry's story.

An interested party was in my office one day trying to buy my corporation. As they left I became dizzy, collapsed to the floor, and lost consciousness. And that is the last thing I remember for months. I had suffered a stroke."

Mrs. Grimbolt gasped, but Lillian remained stoic.

"Only the medical records indicate how long I remained unconscious. I, myself, do not remember. After months, nearly a year, of lying in a vegetative state, I suddenly awoke to hear voices around my bed. After several days, my head cleared, although I could not speak or move the left side of my body. A physical therapist took special interest in my 'case.' Many more weeks passed, or maybe it was months. I don't know. Unexpectedly, one day while I was exercising, I felt sensations in my paralyzed arm and leg, and as subsequent weeks passed, my mind became more acute. That was the turning point in my convalescence. Of the many burning desires in my mind, the most prevalent, and it carried me through many discouraging days, was to escape the nursing home. Not that I was abused or mistreated. I just felt I was not finished with contributing to society.

"Kathy Carson was the nursing home physical therapist. She was a motivator who greatly encouraged me. It was through the association with her that I met her family."

Neither lady made a comment, so he went on.

"My second day out of the nursing home was the day I met you, Mrs. Grimbolt. I know I looked terrible with someone else's cast-off clothes, mismatched shoes, and my untidy appearance, but you accepted me, and I will always appreciate you. I have many people to thank for my recovery, but foremost I thank God."

Both ladies were solemn and quiet as he continued.

"Mrs. McKenzie, you have gone way beyond merely accepting me as an employee. You are one of the most generous and accepting people I have met. It all began with Mrs. Grimbolt. I owe you two so much. Neither words nor money can repay the encouragement and trust you both have shown in me. Whatever enterprises I have recently undertaken, I owe the success to you. Now you know why I feel that I'm taking advantage of you, Lillian. I'm sorry for deceiving you both. You have every right to release me from my employment. In fact, I'll begin packing now." With that, he got up from his chair and started for the door.

"Sit down, Harry!" It was Lillian. She was the first to recover. He obeyed her like a child. "You didn't tell half of it. I know all about you. I've heard from at least two sources. You are the most remarkable person I've ever met and I greatly admire you. I'll tell Sadie all about your return from the point of no return. Now go back to work! Undoubtedly, we'll hear more about this extraordinary story."

Harry excused himself.

He felt exhausted from spilling his guts, so to speak, relating what he thought only he and very few others knew. He staggered out with a strong desire to talk with Kathy.

He was getting very busy with his projects, and he either needed to quit something like Mrs. McKenzie's work or get more help. The kids were doing a great job. No complaints there. The recent car transportation endeavor was taking a lot of time, not only contracting with dealerships but also scheduling the drivers. If he had a good person he could rely on and share the responsibility with, it would take a lot of pressure off him. His body responded to his every demand, but he was aware of the consequences of overload. What started with a small complimentary work place in a corner had grown to a leased two room office suite still within the auto dealership.

One day he was sitting at his desk working at the computer making a schedule for drivers and arranging pick-ups. He had advertised for a secretary and had interviewed several that morning. It was nearly lunchtime, but there was one more scheduled applicant who suddenly appeared, stuck her head in the door, and inquired, "Hello, is this where I make application for work?"

Harry's concentration was broken, his head jerked up, and his pen tumbled to the floor. His back was to the voice and he held on to the computer desk with both hands.

"What is it you want?" He said, his voice weak, but he had to be sure.

"You advertised for a reliable hand, and I'm your person."

He thought he recognized that voice or had heard one just like it. He had to be certain. Perhaps a few more responses would clear the memory.

"What makes you think you can do the job?"

"I'm not exactly sure, but my father taught me how to work. I worked my way through school and I'm not afraid to learn something new. If I don't do a good job, I'll be the first to know it and I'll resign."

So far he liked what he heard. One more question. "What kind of business did your father have?"

"He had the biggest and best medical laboratory in town. You've probably heard of him, Harry Tucker."

He swung his chair around slowly, afraid to believe his ears, hoping … anticipating … Each froze as time stood still. Father and long-separated daughter stared at each other. Moments passed before reality set in. Entangled arms, sobs, and happy voices all mingled as father and daughter were astonishingly, unbelievably reunited.

"I thought you were in Europe?"

"I thought your were dead!"

"I didn't know how to contact you. I called the laboratory. The person who answered was one I did not recognize, and she did not know you."

"Your brother has not kept me informed of anything, and he has been out of touch," Harry moaned.

"With me also," Heather said.

It took them a while to gain composure and catch their breath.

"I have a long story to tell, and I know you're anxious to hear about the events that have transpired in your absence. I dropped from society about two or three years ago," he said as he switched on the this voice mail.

Arm in arm the ecstatic father and daughter, both hearts bursting with love, departed the building and headed for a restaurant where they could have a relaxed lunch and start bringing each other up to date.

"I wrote letter after letter to you, Dad, even after you stopped answering."

"That must have been about the time I had the stroke."

"The one time Thomas telephoned, he told me about that and said you would never recover. That you were as good as dead and not responding to anyone or anything. It sounded as if he thought you would die. But he told me not to come. He promised to call me again but never did."

Harry sat listening to Heather relate the painful anxiety she had experienced. He admired her pretty oval face, her peachy skin, brown eyes she got from her father, the aquiline nose, and the widow's peak she inherited from her mother and which she had always despised as a growing child. Now the long dark hair was pulled back into a French twist. She *looks so much like her mom*, he thought. *She's beautiful.*

Harry related the nightmarish experience of his collapse in his office, the loss of all ability to control bodily functions, including mental and physical. He told of his miraculous recovery and of his renewed faith in his Maker. Heather knew this was an abbreviated version and details would follow.

"How long have you been back? Where are you staying? Thomas sold our house, I hear. He sold my business as well," said Harry.

Heather jumped right in, "I arrived three days ago, and I'm staying at Tom's, but I've only seen him once for about one minute. He seems to be possessed with work and making money. I can't stay with him; he's changed too much. That's one reason I answered the ad in the paper."

"What's the other?" Harry wanted to know.

"I have no money left from the scholarship. I had ten dollars when I landed and I have only change left in my pocket. If you had not persisted in sending me off with a round-trip ticket, I would be there still. Thank you for sending money. I surely missed it when it stopped coming. Guess that must have been about the time you got sick."

Heather would eventually know how Thomas took the house, the business, all his assets and left Harry with only his name that for many months he could neither remember nor speak. She would learn of her father's struggle to convalesce, to regain his mental status, and how he became productive again.

"Well, do I get the job? You haven't said."

They were back in the office and Harry had explained what the work entailed.

"I haven't seen your application yet," he teased. "It's my bet you are overqualified."

"Dad!" she tried to sound perturbed. It was good to hear his humor again.

That sounds so good, he thought. *Dad*. He had longed to hear that title and to be a father again to this precious gift. She had worked for him in her teen years, and he knew she would be an asset to him now.

"When can you start?"

"Right now!"

There wasn't much time left in the work day, and he was more interested in celebrating than in working, but he briefly explained how she could use the computer to move vehicles from point A to point B, C, and so on. Once she saw the complete picture, he knew she could operate the business on her own.

"How did you get here today?"

"Walked," she answered flatly. "I have been walking from place to place all day making applications for employment. I am practically penniless."

"Doesn't Thomas have an extra car?"

"He wasn't overly hospitable."

"Where's your baggage. At Thomas'?"

"I didn't feel comfortable there."

As Harry locked up, Heather said, "My sole possessions are right here," indicating the shoulder bag she had placed on his desk. "Thomas must have let all my things go when he sold our home."

"We're both starting over," Harry said as he ushered her to his parked pickup.

"I'm sorry about you losing everything. I wish I hadn't gotten sick."

"I wish you had not taken ill, but what Tom did is not your fault, Dad, and don't feel bad about that. Thomas and I used to be so close. I just wonder what's happened to him."

"I'll try to make it up to you," Harry said thoughtfully.

"Dad, don't worry. I am so thankful to have found you. I was worried sick and didn't know where to start my search. God is so good to me … us. He answered my prayer and directed me to you. It's a miracle."

"Amen. He's good to everyone! I wish more people would take time to show their appreciation. I'm temporarily living in a run-down apartment on the edge of town. Across the tracks, you might say. There's no hot water, but the 'outhouse' is functional when the inside plumbing breaks. It's well stocked with catalogues," he said, not looking at his daughter.

She raised her eyebrows, *wondering to what kind of place he was taking her. My poor father*, she was thinking. *He suffered worse than I have imagined. He has had a pretty rough time. No matter*, she thought. *As long as we are together, we will both be happy.* When they pulled up in front of the McKenzie mansion and pressed a remote control, and as the big awesome iron gates swung open, she gulped and let her mouth hang open. In awe of the surroundings, she had no time to question him about his seeming familiarity with the place. When she finally found her voice, she said, "Some apartment house 'across the tracks.'"

"You haven't seen the apartment yet," he reminded her.

They saw Mrs. McKenzie walking amongst her flowers, and he stopped the truck. He got out and walked over to her, motioning for Heather to follow.

"Hello, Boss Lady." She was always amused when he called her by that title. He cleared his throat and took on a very serious expression.

"Today I met this nice young lady who doesn't have a home to go to, so I told her she could stay with me. It that all right with you?"

Who is this person? Heather thought bewilderedly. *Why is he asking her?*

"Wh-, you, sh-," Lillian stuttered. "Harry, don't play games with me. What's this all about?"

Both Heather and Lillian looked confused.

"Like I said, ma'am, this young, good-looking lady can't go home. She doesn't have a place to stay. This afternoon I accepted her application to work for me. I figured if she lived with me, we could share transportation until she gets on her feet. Didn't you say I could use the house like my own?"

"Why, ye-, yes, I did, but, but HARRY!"

Lillian's exasperation was showing. Heather glanced at her father. She saw humor twinkling in his eyes.

"Mrs. McKenzie, I kid you not, this poor penniless girl is a student who has been attending to studies in Europe and who has no place to call home."

Harry turned to Heather, who, a bit sheepishly, was looking intently at Mrs. McKenzie. Lillian took a step closer to get a better look in the gathering darkness. A look of recognition registered on her face, and she cuffed Harry on the shoulder.

"Mrs. McKenzie, I am happy to introduce to you, my daughter, Heather. Heather, this is my Boss Lady, Mrs. McKenzie."

Lillian reached out, grabbed Heather in a bear hug, kissed her on both cheeks, patted her back, and turned to Harry, who was smiling broadly.

"Harry, whatever am I going to do with you?"

To Heather she said, "This man in as ornery as they come. Remind me to take a belt to him first thing in the morning. Take her things to your house, Harry. I want Heather to come with me for a minute."

"Yes, ma'am," he smiled, trying to look whipped.

"It's nice to meet you, Mrs. McKenzie."

"Call me Lillian, everyone does."

"This whole situation is a complete surprise to me. Dad was telling me about his run-down apartment house on the edge of town when he abruptly pulled into this gorgeous compound. I still don't know what's going on here."

"Your dad will tell you himself. Tell me about you."

"As Dad said, I've just returned from study in Europe. Actually, I spent time in several countries studying under well-known masters of music. I now need work, so I followed up on a newspaper ad for employment and it was my father advertising for help. It was the shock of my life to see him under such peculiar circumstances. I thought I had lost him." Heather left the thought hanging, not knowing how much she should say to Lillian.

Lillian, seeing the sensitivity and genuineness of this pretty daughter of Harry's, interjected, "Your dad was lost. Lost to an illness that conquers most people. Lost in a system that would intimidate all but a few. Your father is a most remarkable man, and I admire him greatly. Something must be done about it!"

Heather wasn't sure what this last comment meant and didn't have time to ask, as her father entered the room.

"I've enjoyed talking with Heather. Now I know there's at least one nice person in your family."

He smiled at her mock indignation. "We've got a lot of catching up to do, so if you will excuse us, we'll go now," he said.

Goodbyes were exchanged, and Harry escorted Heather to their "home across the tracks."

They talked until early morning when Harry yawned, stretched, and gave Heather a final good-night hug, saying, "It's so good to have you with me. There was a time when I thought I'd never see you again, much less provide you a home."

Chapter Twenty

The few remaining days of the week passed quickly. Heather had more than fulfilled her father's every expectation in helping with the business. Her organizational abilities were taxed and her patience overextended, but she soon had the computer and scheduling under control.

At church her first weekend home, Heather was greeted by some acquaintances from high school and college days. The church service was about to begin when she entered the sanctuary and saw Harry halfway up on the left side sitting toward the middle of a pew. She excused herself as she stepped on someone's toe to get to her father's side, where she assumed he had saved a seat for her. She then saw two kids, one on either side of him. Their closeness told her she would not be under his arm that day.

Harry gave her a shy smile as he leaned over to say, "This is Paul," and, pointing to the girl on his other side, "Meet Sari. These are my young friends."

The service commenced, and with some embarrassment she noted a bit of jealousy surfacing within. Her first thought was, *Who are these kids taking my father's attention*? But then she quickly remembered scenes from earlier days when kids were drawn to him.

After the final "amen" was pronounced and they filed outside, she noticed a woman who was obviously the children's mother, glancing her way rather nervously and walking toward her with an uncertain smile playing around the corners of her mouth. Heather also noticed the woman's well-shaped body and shiny black hair. The closer Kathy came, Heather's attention was drawn to something extraordinary in her facial features. It was the unusual color of the woman's eyes.

"Hello, I'm Kathy Carson. I apologize for my children taking your place beside your father today. They seem to think he's their private property."

Heather got a better look at Kathy's strikingly violet-colored eyes, flawless complexion, and liked her warm personality.

"I'm Heather. No offense taken, he has an affinity for children." *I wonder what her relationship is to my father*, she was thinking when Kathy spoke again.

"The children and I would like to invite you and your father to lunch today." Harry stepped up just as Kathy finished extending the invitation.

"Dad, Mrs. Carson has just invited us to lunch with her family."

Without hesitation Harry accepted, giving Heather a comforting smile as he laid a fatherly arm across her shoulders.

While the food was being prepared for the table, Heather sat with Paul and Sari in the living room talking about school and related activities. She liked the children. Soon the food was ready, and they sat down to an enjoyable meal and lively conversation.

After lunch the two women washed the dishes while Harry and the children took their leave to the family room.

Kathy looked seriously at Heather and said, "You have a perfect right to be protective of your father."

"What do you mean?" The question caught Heather off guard.

"You are the apple of his eye, and I know he loves you dearly. He speaks of you with great affection. In fact, when your dad was so sick in the nursing home, you were the one he wanted to see. You were the one he asked for."

"What is your relationship to my father?"

The directness of the question temporarily shook Kathy. *Much like her father*, she thought as she formed an answer.

"Your father was admitted to the nursing home where I work as a rehabilitation physical therapist. My first encounter with him revealed nothing unusual for his condition. He presented as the typical stroke patient with complete one-sided paralysis. His face was deformed because of paralysis, and he had the usual look of despair in his eyes. Progress notes in his chart indicated he had not responded in any way to verbal or physical stimuli for months. He was transferred to a rehabilitation hospital after his initial admission to the trauma center. At that place they did all they could, but for all their programs, Harry's condition did not improve." She watched Heather carefully, wondering if she should continue in graphic terms.

Heather said, "please continue."

"He was then transferred to the rehab nursing home where I work. The doctor ordered the usual therapies; speech and physical. After several weeks of treatments, on one particular follow-up visit, I detected a slight change in his muscle tone. This would be normal for the healthy side of his body. As I looked into his face to tell him my findings, I saw an intensity rarely exhibited in stroke victims. I looked into his eyes and I saw not the blankness commonly seen in people with brain attacks but something that told me that behind those eyes there was still an intelligent, restless human being wanting to be released. I'm sorry to say your brother was very impatient with him."

With this Kathy paused, not wanting to offend Heather by talking negatively about her brother in this manner.

"It's all right, Kathy, Thomas has changed to such an extent that I don't even know him anymore."

Kathy continued. "It's impossible to predict the degree of rehabilitation stroke patients can achieve, therefore the doctor could not give Thomas any hope. Thomas became impatient, relegated your father to lost humanity, took his business, real estate, including the family home, and all other possessions." Kathy paused, looking embarrassed. "I'm sorry. I don't mean to be uncomplimentary about your brother. I do not know his character, only what has happened with respect to your father."

Heather thought she noted personal feelings here.

"Please don't feel the need to apologize. Thomas has become a mystery to both my father and me," Heather said and urged Kathy to continue.

"On subsequent follow-up treatments your father seemed to comprehend what I said and made every effort to follow instructions while I exercised him. Then one day while the doctor, nurse, your brother and his attorney, the social worker, and I were in his room evaluating your father's condition, I had the shock of my life. I immediately realized he did not have complete aphasia and that he comprehended what was being said. He certainly understood the opinions expressed by the evaluation team!"

The women had finished cleaning the kitchen and were now seated at the kitchen table, sipping cups of hot herbal tea.

"What made you think he understood the situation?" Heather asked.

"I was leaning lightly against the bed with my back to Harry. For several minutes I had been trying to give my appraisal of Harry's condition, but every time I thought it was appropriate to enter the discussion, I was interrupted. The dialogue became heated, with no attention being given to the patient. Just when I started to offer my assessment again, I felt a movement on my side. I turned around and saw Harry's extended paralyzed hand where I was leaning. I don't know if it was the look in his eyes or a slight movement of his head, but I knew he did not want me to voice my opinion. I remained quiet."

"How long have you been in love with my father?"

Stunned, Kathy felt a heat wave coming on. Looking into those direct, honest eyes of Heather's, Kathy had to divert her own.

With downcast eyes she whispered, "I didn't think it was that apparent."

"Only another woman could see it," Heather responded, trying to smile. She did not know very much about this lady and did not want to encourage a relationship just yet but she liked her.

Heather was very protective of her father. Many women had tried to form a close bond with him in her growing-up years, but she and Thomas prevented this every chance they got. She recalled with pleasure the methods she and her brother used.

"Your father, being a typical man, doesn't have a clue, so please don't say anything. I would be terribly embarrassed."

Very sensitive, Heather thought as the others traipsed in to see what was going on. Only Harry wondered about the pink hue to Kathy's countenance.

Paul and Sari took an immediate liking to Heather. Paul, being thirteen now, was in that hate/love mode with girls. He found it most perplexing to be around Heather. He liked her very much and wanted her to like him, but he just did not know what to say or how to say it. It seemed that his "tange got all tongled up" when trying to talk in her presence. He wondered if she would have the same interest in his "creations" as did her father. *Probably not, she's a girl*, he thought. He wanted to show her his inventions just the same.

"Mommy, do you think we could go to the zoo?" Sari asked.

"I have season's passes, if everyone would like to go," Kathy agreed, and a little later everyone piled into her van.

They enjoyed a pleasant ride to the zoo, everyone chatting and laughing. Paul was sitting next to Heather, which was both horrible and wonderful. He tried to squeeze closer to the window. Heather recognized his uneasiness and suspected the cause. She put her arm up over his shoulders and pulled him toward her, saying, "Are you afraid of me, Paul? I won't bite, I'm a vegetarian like my dad." Needless to say, Paul turned crimson, and the wind coming through his opened window did not help a bit to cool his face.

Heather had an infectious laugh, one that made you want to laugh too. No one saw the interchange, except Sari. She seemed always around when he was embarrassed. She did not tease him about it, for she sensed his discomfort and did not want to make it harder for him. Heather was distracted by something her dad was saying but continued to keep her arm loosely around Paul's shoulders. He got used to it after a while.

After a pleasant time observing the many different animals and laughing at their playful antics, they returned home. It was dusk but not too late for Heather to see Paul's fabrications. How should he ask her? Kathy went inside to make popcorn and a fruit salad.

"Heather, I bet Paul would love to show you some of the things he's made," suggested Harry. "He's a good hand at making anything you need. I want to show you the ZYCLE he made for me. Without it, I would have had a far, far more difficult time getting the exercise I needed to convalesce."

Paul ducked his head at the nice compliment. "Thank you, Harry" was all he could say. He was thinking how nice it was for Harry to invite Heather to view his works. It saved him from looking directly at her.

"I would like very much to see what you are up to," said Heather and continued, "Remember the things I used to make, Dad? When you were in your shop working, I had to be right with you so you put me to pounding nails even though I was too young to make anything. You helped me make several useful things during my childhood. I wonder whatever happened to the birdhouse I made and hung in the maple tree in our backyard."

"That was one of your first attempts at building, and you did a good job of it," Harry said, praising his daughter.

The more Paul verbalized about things common to him, the easier it was to talk with this pretty lady. Heather recognized his ability to construct usable articles out of otherwise worthless materials.

"You're a genius, Paul Carson," said Heather, "Someday I'll hear how famous you have become. I'll read about you in the newspaper. What are your aspirations?"

Paul had not shared his most recent dream with anyone, but he felt that his innermost thoughts were safe with Heather.

"Since making a device that helped Harry … ah, I mean your dad … well, actually, from the very beginning, I felt really uncomfortable calling your dad by his first name, but that's what he insisted on. Mom wants me to be very respectful of older people. Maybe I should call you Miss Heather."

They both laughed and she said, "You better not! I understand what you are saying, Paul. Lillian wants me to call her by her first name, too, but it's hard to do. You were talking about your future plans," Heather encouraged.

"Call her Queen Lillian. That's what Sari started. It's easy and respectful."

"You're wise beyond your years."

"Well, since seeing how someone can truly benefit from specialized appliances like the ZYCLE I made for your dad, I've thought maybe I could be an inventor for medical devices or study to be a physiatrist."

"What's that?"

"A physiatrist is one who treats physically and orthopedically handicapped people to help get their bodies working again. This is done by using physical therapy with related aids."

"You have high goals, and I know you can reach them. I think we never reach high enough. We usually shortchange our God-given abilities."

"You believe in God, don't you, H-Heath- … Heather." There, he finally said it. He had been having difficulty getting it out, for some reason. Just saying her name made him feel more comfortable and confident.

"Yes, Paul, I've always believed in God. He has been my security, my friend, and companion. I'm thankful Dad has recently found Him in a more personal way, too. I think you and your sister have been contributing factors."

They were interrupted by Sari calling them for an evening snack.

"Thanks for looking at my stuff."

"You're a cool guy and you'll go far. I want to thank you again for helping my father. He says without you and your family, he would still be in the nursing home."

"I really like your dad. I've never had one, but he is what I'd want a father to be."

They were at the door. Heather turned, looked at Paul, and said, "He's been the best dad I could have ever hoped for" and gave Paul another hug. He could barely keep his feet on the floor as they entered the house.

Chapter Twenty-One

Something was going on, and Harry could not put his finger on it. Mrs. McKenzie had become a different person since her talk with Kathy several months ago. She seemed more settled and a lot happier. There was less of a rough edge to her voice and demeanor, or was it his imagination? Rumors circulated that she had been having serious and heartfelt conversations with Mrs. Grimbolt, who now attended church regularly. They both were going to be baptized in a few weeks. But, no, it was something besides joining a church. Usually, he was involved when plans were being made. No one's birthday was approaching that he could think of. He noticed covert glances his way from time to time from little groups of close friends, but definitely felt he was on the outside of this situation.

Harry was on his feet now, financially speaking. All of his businesses were prospering. *It is incredible what the Lord has allowed me to do*, he mused one day as he observed Heather with the telephone stuck on one ear and both hands flying across the computer keys. She not only had the automobile transportation under control but also had generated several more clients, thanks largely to her winsome personality. He had hired Larry, former nursing home maintenance man, to take charge of his private landscaping service.

Harry had been a registered medical laboratory technologist. Along with all his other important cards in his billfold, his licenses to practice were missing. It had taken months to process applications and forms necessary to re-establish his registry. Harry was able to obtain continuing education and laboratory refresher courses from the local hospitals. He was enrolled at the university for an evening course in computer science. He was now once again in the process of opening a clinical medical laboratory, an operation with which he was familiar. He was happy and felt good about his body's return to health. His recent medical checkup showed a strong heart and a low blood cholesterol level. There was no indication of any more problems with hypokalemia, low potassium blood level, or anything else. The only exception was his cholesterol level, but when he exercised regularly, it stayed under control. The only indication of a previous stroke was a slight limp and a ptosis or drooping of the left eyelid, which was barely noticeable even to close friends who were aware of his medical history.

This evening he was taking Kathy and her children out to eat at a local Italian restaurant whose reputation boasted delicious food. The entire Carson family enjoyed the Italian cuisine. He was not only hungry but eager to be with her. Any pretense was acceptable as long as he could be with Kathy. He was not a little mixed up about his emotions where she was concerned, however. Each time she was near, he felt long subdued emotions deep within. He chided himself for his foolishness. Eight or ten years is a considerable age difference, although he did not know her exact age. When she turned her beautiful violet-colored eyes on him, he could feel tingles that started in his feet and continued all the way up his body, bounced off his brain, and finally settled comfortably around his heart.

Maybe I could talk to Heather about it. No, children and young adults are supposed to talk with their parents about such personal matters. Parents are supposed to be mature enough to make educated, rational decisions and maintain control of their emotions. But this is about the heart. Doesn't that qualify? No, these are foolish thoughts, he said to himself. *Besides I've seen it many times. When a health care worker plays a major role in helping a patient get well, the patient often substitutes emotion for gratefulness.* That was his circumstance, he decided, and prepared for the "appointment." His mind was at odds with his heart.

They met at the restaurant at the appointed time and were immediately ushered to a table.

"Where are Paul and Sari? In the bathroom?" Harry asked. He liked the children, and besides, he felt less apprehensive when they were with them.

"I, ah, ah, took them to the library," Kathy stammered. "What shall we order? I am really hungry," she said, hoping to change the subject.

"Are they doing a research project?" he persisted.

"Yes, I gave them one." Kathy appeared to be nervous.

She has a lot on her mind, being a single parent with so many responsibilities, he thought.

"What are they working on?" Harry inquired.

"Harry …" *This is not going to be easy*, she thought.

The pause caused him to look into her face. *Uh-oh*, he thought, *she's got something serious on her mind.* He had been around her long enough to interpret that expression. *Just as I thought; I've gotten too close to her. Dumpville, here I come. Dumpville? Where did that come from? She can't dump me, I am not hers.* To think of that immediately gave him a feeling of sadness. *What is wrong with me, all these emotions I'm having, hope I am not heading for a relapse. Maybe I am at the age for fantasizing. Got to get some fresh air.*

"Harry." The waiter was standing by the table, pad in hand waiting for their order.

The food arrived, and they bowed their heads and gave thanks.

"I believe you said 'Harry' a couple of times," he said around forks full of spaghetti. How long have we known each other?" she asked.

"Well, let's see, including time in the nursing home, well over two years, maybe."

"Nearly three years!"

"That so?" His responses were short when he was nervous, and his heart was in his throat. "Paul and Sari have really grown. A lot has happened to both of us."

Men can be so slow, she thought. *How am I going to say this to him? I do not want to drive him away. The children adore him so, and I …* She was having trouble putting her thoughts into words as she picked up her fork and spoon and commenced rolling the spaghetti, but mostly she pushed the food around on her plate. The longer they sat, the more anxious she became.

"Can I get something else for you?" the waiter interrupted her thoughts.

"Some dessert?" Harry asked, hoping to delay the drop of the bombshell.

"No, thank you."

The meal was over, the check arrived, and she still had not emptied her heart. Outside they stood by her car.

"It's a nice evening. Do you have a few minutes before you need to pick up the children?" he asked. "Can we take a walk?"

"Yes, that would be nice."

"There's a small park just a block away. Would you care to take a stroll around it?"

"Love to," she said, hoping for time to muster her courage. They walked to the park.

"Is this where you were mugged?"

"No, this is a safer one."

They took a slow, leisurely walk along the shrub-lined pathway. The walkway had been specifically designed for the purposes of quiet strolls such as they were doing now. During daylight hours, he had often seen people jogging here. Harry's hand occasionally brushed hers.

If she knew how I feel about her, she would crown me.

"Harry?"

Here it comes. He tensed.

"Yes?"

"You're getting along really well, aren't you? You have convalesced almost completely."

"The Lord has blessed."

"What's in your future? More business ventures?"

"You know, Kathy, I've been thinking about that. Just what do I want out of the remainder of my life? I suppose you think of your future, too, but your children dictate yours to a degree."

"Yes, they do. I'll be working my fingers to the bone getting them through school. Paul now wants to be a doctor. You've inspired him, you know, and it's your fault if he goes to medical school."

She turned slightly toward him, offering him a sweet smile and hoping the ambiguity of the statement would ease her tension. He wanted to reach for her hand to give it a comforting squeeze. She was looking particularly lovely this evening. Her shiny, satiny black hair and her gorgeous porcelain complexion glowed in the twilight.

"You are a well-educated professional woman doing a wonderful job with your patients. Your children see that, no doubt. You are an excellent example to them."

Her rephrased questions broke into his thoughts.

"Where would you like to be in ten years?"

"The Lord gives various abilities to everyone, some more than others. He has given me the ability to do business. Somewhere I have to draw the line, though, for He says to do all things in moderation. I think I'll remain status quo for a couple of years until the laboratory shows profits. Then I'll probably let Larry have the landscaping business for little or nothing. If Heather wants to manage the auto transportation, perhaps I'll do the same for her." She will still want to pursue music, I'm sure. Probably part-time."

"You're the most generous, selfless person I know."

"Eventually, with the money we get from liquidating a company, we can start a scholarship fund for kids from hard-working families who need a little help. I've always thought of doing that."

Kathy gulped, and he spontaneously grabbed her arm.

"Are you all right?" he asked.

"Y-yes, just fine," she said. "That's very unselfish of you to want to do that. What made you decide that?"

"I have recently met some wonderful kids who are made from excellent fabric and whose mom is hard-working."

Again, the gasp, but Harry was holding on. "I believe the principle is, 'freely you have received, freely give.' Can't improve on God-given directions, now, can we?"

"Harry, you are a really nice, generous, compassionate, and certainly well-loved man. Loved by kids, let alone all your employees and those who demand your attention after church each week. I have noticed older women like you too," she smiled.

Harry continued, "Since I was a teenager, I have thought of being involved with orphanages, too. I would love to go to a war-ravaged or developing country and visit homes for abandoned children and try to help them. My heart goes out to them. How would you like to do that?"

He almost came to a stop, wondering how she might take that comment. *I wonder why I feel so self-conscious about some things I say.*

"I think that is a wonderful God-inspired project. Those parentless children would stick to you like glue. Knowing your love for children and theirs for you, I would say you would either have to stay with the orphanage or you would have to bring the whole school back home with you."

Her heart softened for this man who did not comprehend his own kindhearted, compassionate character. These attributes he wore like skin. They were bonded to him.

They had arrived back at her van, and he feared what was coming. He had done all he could do to prevent eminent doom.

"Nice of you to say so," Harry said.

"I mean it!"

"God's good to me."

She had her van door open, waiting to get in, but he saw her hesitation as she tried to put her thoughts to words. He did not want to pressure her by asking what was on her mind because he feared what might be coming. Guessing she would wait until another time, he closed her door, took a step back, gazed at her, and heard, "Harry, I love you!"

Talk about being stunned! He stood like a stone statue looking dumb and confused. He had the same rush he experienced months ago when her soft whisper graced his ear. *Am I having another stroke?* he thought.

Kathy took his reticence as a negative response and sped away, not wanting him to see her embarrassment and tears. In her rearview mirror she saw him still standing like a statute staring after her.

Several days passed. Many times he tried reaching Kathy by telephone. He needed desperately to know what she meant and to clarify what she said. With impaired hearing it was hard to tell what his mind perceived and what his ears received. Had he heard correctly? While his hearing was slightly impaired, by closely watching lips, he usually had no trouble understanding. Could he have mistaken her motives at the restaurant and on their walk in the park? Something had been on her mind all evening. She was not one to appear anxious or restless, and she was well-dressed for having worked all day. Could she have dressed up for him, he wondered. Every scenario he thought of left him perplexed.

The next day he was still unsettled. *She appreciates me for spending time with her children and that's that!* he stormed at himself. *Heather! Where's Heather, I'll talk to her. No*, he thought, *that would be embarrassing.*

Heather returned in a few minutes from a break and saw her father in deep thought, in fact, he did not even acknowledge her speaking.

"Hello, anybody in there?" she asked while tapping on his head.

"Heather, what do you know about lo-..." He faltered.

"What? Lo- who?"

"Oh, nothing. Nevermind."

"Business?"

"You might say that."

"Are you in trouble?"

"Only in my mind."

"I saw Kathy at the coffee shop with someone."

That's it, he thought, *she wanted to tell me about her boyfriend. She's so lovely, it is a wonder she has not become attached before this. Hope he likes the children.*

"Have you two had a fight?" Heather's question brought him back to reality.

"Nothing to fight about." He sounded depressed.

"Dad, we have to talk! I really love you, but you are a man, and I have to help you understand something. Remember when you used to take me aside, hold my hand, or put an arm around me, and say, 'Some things in life are hard to learn, but you'll understand when you're older.' Remember that?"

"Many times. Did you have hard lessons to learn?"

"Yes, but now I'm wondering how old one has to be before he's learned anything!" she shrugged with a smile. She gave him an affectionate hug, kissed him on the cheek, lifted his chin, and said, "I've never said anything like this to you, either to your face or behind your back, so please don't take it disrespectfully, for I'd never say anything to hurt you, OK?"

He nodded.

She continued as she backed toward his office door, "Dad, you are positively, incontrovertibly, and unequivocally dense! In some things you are as slow as molasses oozing uphill on a cold day in January."

She was gone, and now he was more confused than ever. *Wonder what she meant by all that,* he wondered.

Now knowing Kathy had a friend, Harry stayed away. In fact, he found it convenient to visit other area churches just to avoid seeing her on weekends. Kathy thought he was intentionally avoiding her. With schedules full, church was the only time he could depend on visiting with the family. He had not been invited to the Carson home since that dreadful experience several weeks earlier. One afternoon while hurrying to answer the telephone before the answering machine picked up, he was startled to hear, "Harry?" His heart skipped a beat.

"Yes?"

"This is Kathy."

"It's good to hear your voice again." His rich baritone sounded good to Kathy, too.

"Would you have a little time for me?" she asked timidly.

"I'm sorry I made you angry. I've missed you."

He thought he heard a break in her voice. By now he was standing, subconsciously thinking his body language could convey the message he wanted her to get.

"Harry, you don't have to say anything. I'm the one to apologize, and I have a request."

He could not get his mouth into gear. He just stood making facial expressions and spastically waving his arms.

Kathy continued, feeling awkward with the silence at his end of the telephone.

"You've often mentioned that you are thankful that I was in some small way able to help you when you were ill. You also asked if ever there was something you could do for me to just ask…. . Hello, are you still there?"

"Yes." A weak response.

"Will you do something for me?"

Harry cleared his throat several times, trying to get words around an obstruction.

"Kathy, I'd fly to the moon for you, get a package of green cheese, and personally deliver it."

"My request is equally as difficult." The strained conversation ended with Harry wondering what he was getting into. He also wondered how the telephone cord got over one shoulder and wound around his neck and between his knees. He was standing on one foot.

Harry, being intrinsically shy, did not like crowds, especially if he had some public part to play. It's a wonder he ever succeeded in business, but he tried to make his contacts one-on-one or in small groups.

From what he could recall, besides being overjoyed at hearing her voice again, she wanted him to go to some awards convention. And she said something about Mrs. McKenzie. But that's not surprising, he thought. Boss Lady was always having a tea, a party, or a convention of some kind.

Harry was waiting by the entrance to the civic auditorium when he spotted friends coming up the walk. As soon as Paul got a glimpse of Harry, he sprinted toward him with Sari fast on his heels. They were still hugging and doing high fives when the remaining troupe arrived. It was good to see Mrs. Grimbolt, who was looking for all the world as if she had a secret she could hardly contain. She gave him a hug and a peck on the cheek.

Mrs. McKenzie had obviously softened over the months as a result of talking with Sari and later with Kathy. She was enjoying a growing friendship with God. He got a hug from her, too.

With reserve, Kathy extended her hand, and he took it. It felt warm and fragile. He sensed he held it too long and self-consciously dropped his eyes.

They found their seats with Paul on his left. He looked for Sari on his other side but was surprised to see Kathy sitting there with Sari on her right, and the others, except Mrs. McKenzie, filled up the row.

The auditorium was filling fast and the ceremony was about to begin as Harry leaned over to Kathy and whispered, "What's this all about?" She gave sort of a hunched-up shoulder answer because their attention was diverted to the speaker.

"Where's Mrs. McKenzie?' he asked. Kathy pointed to the podium and put her hand in his. He lost his concentration of the proceedings.

Chapter Twenty-Two

~~~~~~~~~~~~~~~~

Thomas was perplexed. He was also in pain. He was lying on a plush leather sofa with his broken leg elevated. Three days ago while water skiing, he flipped, and somehow in the bedlam and swirling water, he suffered a fractured tibia. The leg was throbbing and the cast was heavy. The ice pack had fallen off, and he was in a dither trying to get comfortable. He had not taken time to consider his surroundings or station in life for a long time. His motto was, "Drive, drive, and drive." Like a military tank, he drove over people, places, and things. Now, laid up as he was, he was forced to reflect on his life and he did not necessarily like what he saw. In fact, he was beginning to realize that his anxiety was a result of him trying to satisfy this urge, this driving passion, this need, this … greed? … am I greedy, he wondered.

Could it actually be greed that was making him behave this way? His dad was very successful and he seemed at peace. Did I get it all wrong, he questioned? The mistakes he had made, the shady business dealings, the people he'd hurt, all came flooding into his confused, mixed up brain. Hard, relentless work, and constant dealings acted as an opiate to his perverted self-centered character.

He had no friends, only several acquaintances who, like him, were only out for themselves. Had he any friends, he would not be alone in this present predicament! Friends. Friends, he recalled, know all about you and still like you. He had heard that description from when he was a youngster. Over the years, who had been his friends? He had to go way back in time. An impression tugged at his brain, he pushed it away. It kept returning. He did not want to dwell on conviction; it crushed his mind. Why didn't the pain pills bring relief? He really needed help, but there was no one to call. Where was Heather, he wondered. Wasn't she here several weeks ago? He presumed she had returned from somewhere in Europe. *She should be here helping me*, he grumbled within. When the pain medicine wore off, impressions haunted his mind again. He could not think clearly.

Thoughts of his dad haunted him. He could not bury them. In utter frustration he gave in to his conscience. "Dad," he screamed! "Dad, I need you!" Great heaves of emotional pain wracked his muddled mind and permeated his entire body. His physical discomfort became nothing. *He was always my best friend. Where is he? What is he? What have I done to my own father? It does not matter in what condition he is—I need him.* Swallowing the bile of selfishness, he wondered what had happened to his dad. He reached for the telephone to give the nursing home a call. His conscience hurt worse than the broken leg. The leg would heal, but his pride did not allow him to complete the call.

His father, the one who had fed him, given him shelter, read bedtime stories, loved him, raised him and Heather almost single-handedly, paid for his education, and who had given him his first job. Had he ever thanked his father? No! His seared conscience smoldered in his head. Why was he sweating? The air conditioner was on, and he did not have a fever. *I have got to talk with someone*, he thought, *but who? My secretary would think I am crazy. The attorney, he would know I am. A pastor. Yes, I will talk to the pastor. But I don't have a pastor. God? Oh, surely not Him.* Thomas had dropped God years ago. He remembered the Christian stories his father had read to him and how warm he had felt to have Jesus as his friend. The experience of thinking Jesus was in his heart was just a feeling, just an emotion. It never developed into a trusting friendship the way it did with Heather. The almighty dollar is what he sought and that is what he got. He would have liked to trade it for some friendship right then.

Why did I have to break this blasted leg anyway? If it were not for this, I would not be having these horrid thoughts. The sweating commenced again. He was wet and cold. No, he was hot, then cold. He wanted a blanket but could not reach it. He could use the crutches, but the pain was horrific when he stood up and the blood rushed down his leg. *Miserable, miserable, miserable is my motto now! God, what am I going to do? God? Did I say God? No way He would listen to me.*

A voice not heard, a presence not seen, but awareness, touched his senses.

Remember the story of David?

Oh, yes, I remember David! What a heathen! Nevertheless, God did so much for him! Talk about protection! He must have been God's pet ... gave him victory over all his enemies ... rich ... he murdered, committed adultery, and broke God's law. Yet, he saw his mistakes and regretted his separation from God. Yes, he was regarded as noble, trustworthy, and a man loved and accepted by God. Yeah, but that was David. It was easier back then.

He will never leave you nor reject you, a small voice said.

I have been too bad. Making money was more important than making relationships.

He will never forgive you, another voice spoke. *How can one person be so without hope?* Finally, to quiet the battle in his mind, he shouted, "God, my heavenly Father, I have really blown it! Thank you for reminding me of the story of David." He thought next of the story of the prodigal son and began to wonder where that story was recorded.

Not only was Thomas in a serious sweat but his tears started flowing. A long-forgotten ability to cry surfaced, and great sobs erupted. Tears and confessions were cleansing his soul. He did not know how long he was in this state. Tears and perspiration were dried when he came to his senses. Only sniffles now. It would take some time to recall every event in detail, but now he was reveling in a warmth he had never experienced before. The leg was not hurting so badly now, and he realized it was long past time to take more medicine. He attempted to rise to make his way to the toilet. As the foot descended, he was prepared for the stabbing pain that usually came, but surprisingly, though it hurt terribly, the pain was tolerable.

In the weeks that followed, he made many changes and formulated new ones. Pride prevented him from doing what he knew he had to do. He had to face his father. It was the hardest thing he had ever thought to do. Harder than apologizing to Mr. Bailey, when, as a child, he stole candy from his store. But he gathered up his courage and went to the nursing home one Sunday morning.

"Not here?" he exclaimed. "Where is he?"

The nurse shrugged. "Haven't heard that name. You sure you're at the right home?"

Oh, no, Thomas thought. *He died and all by himself. No one was with him.* Not expecting his dad to live long, he had prearranged his father's funeral, so it was possible he could have died when Thomas was not available and they had buried him like a pauper. Remorse hung heavily on Thomas.

After several weeks Thomas was back at work, which helped some, but he was plagued by constant, nagging thoughts of his father. Many times during the days to follow, he would recall how hard his dad had worked. Thomas painfully reminisced. *I gave up on him, but he never gave up on me.* On his way home from work one day, the flood of tears was so heavy that he had to pull his car to the roadside and wait until his sobbing subsided. *I took everything he had; his businesses, his home, his money, and his entire life savings.* More tears and remorse followed. "God, what can I do?" *I banished Heather, too, and oh, I need her so much. The way I treated her—she'll never want to see me again. And I don't blame her.* Condemnation and forgiveness competed in battle.

Chapter Twenty-Three

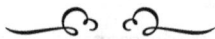

Harry was enjoying being close to Kathy.

"What's Mrs. McKenzie doing up there?" he asked.

"She has something to do with the program."

Mrs. McKenzie was speaking. "Ladies and gentlemen, thank you for coming. You are in for wonderful surprises and a pleasant evening. We have a fantastic program prepared for you that I know you will surely enjoy."

Applause.

"As you know, from year to year, the business community selects a number of entrepreneurs who have shown outstanding performance. Based on business growth, service to other businesses, and giving back to the community in the form of leadership and example, the committee has chosen three extraordinary entrepreneurs."

Another applause. The audience was in a state of expectancy.

"I would now like to introduce last year's finalist, who will announce this year's nominees. Many of you remember Mr. Thomas Tucker."

The audience stood and applauded while Thomas entered from behind the stage and took his position at the podium. Harry gasped and held Kathy's hand so tightly it was beginning to hurt.

"It's OK," she soothed. "Relax and listen."

Thomas pulled the first name from a sealed envelope and announced the name of the third runner-up and then handed the card to the association president, who read of Ms. Sally Wong's business success and her contribution to the community. Sally owned Asian Imports and shared her father's dream of making it big in America. She was only nineteen years old. Her father stayed at home in Korea while sending his daughter to America. "Sank you vetty much," she said, bowed deeply, and returned to her seat in the audience. A burst of applause followed.

As the cheering subsided, Thomas took the card bearing the second name from its envelope. "Mr. James Reed," he called and handed the card to the president. James, fresh out of college three years ago, leased, merged, bought, and sold nursing homes. He was the director of Community Way Rescue Mission and sponsored little league baseball, where he served as a coach. A string of accomplishments was read, and again much applause followed, with some people standing and whistling. The crowd loved him.

Harry had unsettled emotions about people taking credit for God-given skills and abilities.

He lost interest in the proceedings and longed to get out into the fresh air.

Thomas cleared his throat, smiled, and seeming to enjoy the spotlight, tore open the envelope containing the first choice and read the name, "Mr. Harry Tuck-e-r." The name died in his mouth. The president broke in, "Read the name again, please. We didn't hear you." Thomas, white-faced and trembling, handed the card to him. "Mr. Harry Tucker," the president's voice boomed, and Thomas, unnoticed, retreated behind the stage.

Harry sat slouched in his seat, enjoying the feel of Kathy's warm hand in his and paying more attention to her than to the program. He was wondering what this closeness meant, but he was enjoying it too much to shake loose. *Where is her friend? He should be here with her.*

She nudged him. "That was your name he called."

"He what? Must be another by the same name."

"Mr. Harry Tucker, are you in the audience?"

He looked around, confused. He glanced over to Mrs. Grimbolt and then to Mrs. McKenzie, both of whom were beaming and giving him the thumbs up. The announcer began reading from the card. "Mr. Tucker has been chosen the number one entrepreneur of the year for the following reasons: Mr. Tucker was a very successful businessman in this city for many years. Three and a half years ago he suffered a debilitating stroke that left him paralyzed and disfigured. The doctors gave up hope. His companies and home were lost. He was placed on welfare and relegated to a nursing home, where he was to live out his remaining years, a nonentity and in abject misery. A health care provider and her young children took special interest in him, and her twelve-year-old son made a special contraption called a ZYCLE, with which he exercised and regained strength and eventual usage of paralyzed limbs. Perhaps we will see that young man receiving an award here someday," he interjected parenthetically.

"On the very first day after leaving the nursing home, Mr. Tucker found work mowing lawns, which eventually developed into a landscaping service, the Greenway. He and his family were separated. Having been unconscious and in a coma when he entered the nursing home, all identification was stripped from him. Imagine what that would be like. He had to replace all; his driver's license, professional license, social security card, credit cards, money, etc. He then met Mrs. Lillian McKenzie, whom we all know, and became her estate caretaker. Later he employed a group of young boys and girls to wash and clean cars for Mike O'Brien's automobile dealership. Mr. Tucker then saw the need for a system whereby cars could be shuffled from one dealership to another as needs arose. This service has grown to twelve dealerships. He is a leader in his church and contributes to the community's kids' clubs. He is helping young people in his own church raise money to build jungle chapels. He is currently in the process of rebuilding his Medical Clinical Laboratory."

"How did he get all this information?" Harry whispered to Kathy—still in his seat and holding her hand. She urged him to stand, but he refused, being quite adverse to the sequence of events.

He heard Mrs. McKenzie above the applause saying, "Get up, Harry!" She seemed to have a way with him. And with words! He slowly realized the immensity of the occasion and carefully stood to his feet. He was not certain his legs would hold him. He made his way into the aisle, faltered, and took hesitant steps toward the platform, his limp apparent and noticeable. The bright lights and noise from continuous applause dazzled him.

What have I gotten him into? Kathy thought, tears of regret forming, feeling like she had betrayed a true friend. *He has reason to be angry with me now. But it was Mrs. McKenzie who arranged for him to be honored. It had come as a sudden impulse to her ... not uncommon for Lillian*, she remembered.

Lillian admired and greatly respected Harry for his "comeback," as she called it. She had learned from her late husband what it meant to work hard, to be productive, and to give back to society. Never in all her years had she heard such a story as lay within Harry, and she was going to have the whole city know about it or her name was not Lillian P. McKenzie! She had gone to neighbors and to friends and to some of Harry's employees and told them the story. She then went to Mike O'Brien, her most formidable adversary.

He had jumped to conclusions—again—as he was prone to do and shouted, "A cripple? Driving my cars? He can't do that!" and he stormed out of his office, leaving her open-mouthed.

"Get back in here!" she demanded, tapping her cane on the floor and raising her voice as he slammed the door closed. Her raised and assertive voice penetrated the wall. He returned like a disobedient child, and she reminded him of her significant long-standing account, which had established him in the automobile business. She saw him now across the aisle, beaming, shouting, and wildly clapping his hands, head pumping up and down. She nodded her head and returned his full-faced smile.

Paul saw Harry waver and grab the back of an aisle seat. He could not bear to see his friend endure this trauma all by himself. He jumped to his feet, murmuring, "He needs me." Sari heard Paul, and before Kathy could put a restraining hand on her daughter's arm,

Sari was stepping on Paul's heels as he entered the aisle. Mrs. McKenzie took note of this love in action and choked up.

Harry knew Paul and Sari were on each side of him, though his vision was a blur. He felt them there and placed a trembling hand on each young shoulder as he slowly approached the podium. As the great hall slowed its circling, his vision cleared and his mind assumed a semblance of intelligence. The roar of applause was deafening but gradually subsided, and he guessed he should say something. After multiple attempts at clearing his throat, stammering a little to see if his voice was still there, he said simply, "Thank you." The applause exploded again. Then quieted.

Sari was trying to get his attention. He bent toward her and heard her whisper, "Remember the hair in the biscuit? Hang in there."

He smiled and relaxed as he now had something to say. The proximity of the children gave him strength. He said, "Nothing endures without the blessing of God. No one person is a singular success. It takes people, many of them. You can step on them to raise yourself higher than they are, or you can, hand in hand, shoulder to shoulder, walk your way upward." Applause, and the audience was standing.

"Right here on either side of me are prime examples of what I just said. At this moment, they knew when I needed someone to lean on, and without being asked, they came to assist. That's what good business is all about. Helping one another."

More applause.

"As I said, it takes many people for one to become a success. Would my friends please stand?" He paused to try to think of names. It is a good thing he could not, for the entire audience stood, including a multitude of kids. His eyes only saw Kathy waving and smiling shyly. As he descended the stage, both familiar faces along with many people he did not recognize competed to shake hands and offer congratulations. He felt he was going to get beat up by so many pumping his hand and pounding his back. His eyes searched the row where Kathy had been seated. Through fuzzy vision he saw that the whole seating area was vacant. As he looked, he saw why. They were all traipsing down the aisle to meet him. Kathy was leading the way with Heather close behind. Following a little more slowly was Mrs. Grimbolt, who was being assisted by Lillian.

Unheard by ears, but understood by Kathy, Harry mouthed the words, "I love you." He released Paul and Sari and stepped into Kathy's waiting embrace, and two happy, well-blessed hearts beat as one.

Epilogue

—⸎⸎—

Thomas has a rich story to tell, but briefly, he made a complete but tortuous reversal. Money and material things became distasteful to him, and he slowly made amends with his father. The slowness was on his part, not on his dad's. Guilt was unbearable, and his conscience had indelible scars. It was only as he allowed God to forgive him that he found peace and healing. His loving father openly accepted him back into the family, but it was not as easy for his sister.

Information about Strokes

Information relative to a stroke contained in this book is meant for general educational purposes only. Contact your doctor or one or more of the following sources at the end of this section for more detailed information about this condition.

Background

According to the National Institute for Neurological Disorders and Stroke (NINDS), more than 2,400 years ago, the father of medicine, Hippocrates, recognized and described stroke, the sudden onset of paralysis. Stroke was called apoplexy. In 1620 Johann Jakob Wepfer was the first person to suggest that apoplexy, in addition to being caused by bleeding into the brain, could be caused by a blockage of one of the main arteries supplying blood to the brain. Stroke became known as cerebrovascular disease. Today it is called brain attack as well as stroke. Until recently, modern medicine has had very little power over this disease, but the world of stroke medicine is changing, and new and better therapies are being developed every day. Today some people who have a stroke can walk away from the attack with no or few disabilities if they are treated promptly.

Recognition of a Stroke

Symptoms appear suddenly:
- Sudden numbness or weakness of the face, arm, or leg, especially on one side of the body.
- Sudden confusion and trouble talking or understanding speech.
- Sudden trouble seeing in one or both eyes.
- Sudden trouble walking, dizziness, or loss of balance or coordination.
- Sudden severe headache with no known cause.

If you suspect that you or someone you know is experiencing any of these symptoms indicative of a stroke, do not wait, call 911 immediately.

Prevention (Risk Factors)

- **Tobacco**—Smoking increases the risk of stroke. The relative risk of stroke decreases immediately after quitting.
- **Hypertension**—People with high blood pressure have a risk for stroke that is four to six times higher than the risk for those without hypertension. Persistent high blood pressure, pressure greater than 140/90, leads to the diagnosis of hypertension.

- **Diabetes**—People with diabetes have three times the risk of stroke compared to people without diabetes.
- **Heavy alcohol consumption**—This generally leads to high blood pressure.
- **High blood cholesterol levels**—Cholesterol is classified as a lipid. Other lipids include fatty acids, glycerides, alcohol, waxes, steroids, and fat-soluble vitamins A, D, and E.
- **Illicit drug use.**
- **Genetic or congenital conditions.**

Emotional Changes

Stroke patients may have difficulty controlling their emotions or may express inappropriate emotions in certain situations.

Nature's Natural Remedies

Ellen G. White's book *The Ministry of Healing* provides the following natural remedies for increasing one's health on page 127.
- Pure air
- Sunlight
- Moderation in eating
- Rest
- Exercise
- Proper diet
- The use of water
- Trust in divine power

Stroke Resources

Information regarding strokes is free, and you are urged to contact the following organizations:
- American Heart Association – www.heart.org
- The Stanford School of Medicine Stroke Center – www.stanford.edu/group/neurology/stroke/part2.html
- Agatha M. Thrash, MD, Uchee Pines – www.ucheepines.org
- National Stroke Association – www.stroke.org
- National Institute of Health – www.ninds.nih.gov

Please contact the author of this book if you need help finding further resources.
Mahlon F. Harris, mahlonharris@yahoo.com

We invite you to view the complete
selection of titles we publish at:

www.TEACHServices.com

Scan with your mobile
device to go directly
to our website.

Please write or email us your praises, reactions,
or thoughts about this or any other book we publish at:

P.O. Box 954
Ringgold, GA 30736

info@TEACHServices.com

TEACH Services, Inc., titles may be purchased in bulk for
educational, business, fund-raising, or sales promotional use.
For information, please e-mail:

BulkSales@TEACHServices.com

Finally, if you are interested in seeing
your own book in print, please contact us at

publishing@TEACHServices.com

We would be happy to review your manuscript for free.